Responsive Reading

POETS ON POETRY

David Lehman, General Editor
Donald Hall, Founding Editor

New titles

Thom Gunn, *The Occasions of Poetry*
Edward Hirsch, *Responsive Reading*
Philip Larkin, *Required Writing*
James Tate, *The Route as Briefed*

Recently published

John Hollander, *The Poetry of Everyday Life*
William Logan, *All the Rage*
Geoffrey O'Brien, *Bardic Deadlines*
Anne Stevenson, *Between the Iceberg and the Ship*
C. K. Williams, *Poetry and Consciousness*

Also available are collections by

A. R. Ammons, Robert Bly, Philip Booth, Marianne Boruch,
Hayden Carruth, Fred Chappell, Amy Clampitt, Tom Clark,
Douglas Crase, Robert Creeley, Donald Davie, Peter Davison,
Tess Gallagher, Suzanne Gardinier, Allen Grossman, Thom Gunn,
John Haines, Donald Hall, Joy Harjo, Robert Hayden,
Daniel Hoffman, Jonathan Holden, Andrew Hudgins,
Josephine Jacobsen, Weldon Kees, Galway Kinnell, Mary Kinzie,
Kenneth Koch, Richard Kostelanetz, Maxine Kumin,
Martin Lammon (editor), David Lehman, Philip Levine,
John Logan, William Matthews, William Meredith, Jane Miller,
Carol Muske, John Frederick Nims, Gregory Orr, Alicia Ostriker,
Marge Piercy, Anne Sexton, Charles Simic, Louis Simpson,
William Stafford, May Swenson, Richard Tillinghast,
Diane Wakoski, Alan Williamson, Charles Wright,
and James Wright

Edward Hirsch

Responsive Reading

Ann Arbor

THE UNIVERSITY OF MICHIGAN PRESS

Copyright © by the University of Michigan 1999
All rights reserved
Published in the United States of America by
The University of Michigan Press
Manufactured in the United States of America
∞ Printed on acid-free paper

2002   2001   2000   1999   4   3   2   1

A CIP Catalog record for this book is available from the British Library.

Library of Congress Cataloging-in-Publication Data

Hirsch, Edward.
      Responsive reading / Edward Hirsch.
          p.   cm. — (Poets on poetry)
      Collection of previously published essays.
      Contents: The female Yahwist — A fresh hell — Emerson — The
imaginary Irish peasant — Federico García Lorca — Joseph Cornell —
Zbigniew Herbert — Aleksander Wat — Wislawa Szymborska — Philip
Larkin — Derek Walcott — Yehuda Amichai — Donald Barthelme —To
wrestle an angel — My grandfather's poems.
      ISBN 0-472-09692-3 (alk. paper). — ISBN 0-472-06692-7 (paper :
alk. paper)
      1. Poetry—History and criticism.   I. Title.   II. Series.
PN1042.H485   1999
809.1—dc21   99-21650
                                                                  CIP

Preface

The books I love most—poems, stories, essays, novels—are books that have passed through a terrifying silence, that have crossed a murderous divide. They have charted their own course, however perilous, ironic, or unsure, in making their way toward something or somewhere, toward someone. The poet Paul Celan wrote of poems as being en route, as heading "toward something open, inhabitable, an approachable you, perhaps, an approachable reality."

Reading deeply is a matter of deep attention. My own idea of responsive reading—of reading that is engaged, open, lustrous, formative—means going down to a shoreline to find a message in a bottle. It means letting a work of art inhabit your mind and body, transforming yourself into Celan's "approachable you." It means going beyond national borders, sometimes beyond your own language, but it also means going beyond familiar assumptions and ideas—whatever they may be—about a given writer or body of work, at times about the literary enterprise itself. In his *Journals* Ralph Waldo Emerson playfully cites "our accomplished Mrs. B.," who, with a wave of her hand, declares that Transcendentalism means "*A little beyond.*" Mrs. B. presents us with a prospect for reading as well, especially since "a little beyond" also means digging deeper within. "What we need are books that affect us like some really grievous misfortune," Franz Kafka wrote in 1904, "like the death of one whom we loved more than ourselves."

This is a book of encounters and explorations, of discoveries and reconsiderations. Literature is an international enterprise, and one must be an intrepid traveler, crossing geographic, historical, and linguistic borders. In these pieces I envisage writing as a mysterious, oppositional activity, an urgent, oddly self-conscious way of speaking not only to society but also across the frontiers of time. "Beyonding" is a trope, if not for complete transcendence, which is impossible in any case, then at least for a transcendental impulse in reading. The notion of using literature to go further than before, to go past ourselves, seems especially critical at a time when the Emersonian ideal of *creative reading*—of reading as an intimate, triggering, momentous activity—seems endangered in ways that Emerson himself, or Kafka for that matter, could never have suspected.

The essays included in this collection are diverse, but they have, I believe, a certain unity of purpose. I begin with a reconsideration of the "J" author, the most ancient and humanly oriented writer in the Hebrew Bible, and I conclude with a short memoir about my grandfather, whose poems, which have not survived, I have tried to imagine. There is an investigation of a new version of Dante's *Inferno* and a discussion of a splendid biography of Emerson that teaches us to see his darkness, his passion, and his wildness—"the wildness whereof it is spoken," as Frost says—and to recast his work in that light. There are also essays here on a triad of extraordinary Polish poets—Zbigniew Herbert, Aleksander Wat, and Wislawa Szymborska—all of whom write at an acute angle to Polish society, in the margins of official discourse, and struggle mightily to reconcile a metaphysical poetry with a historical one. Nowhere is the writer's fall into time more pronounced than in Eastern Europe.

There is a piece here on the poignant intersection of the personal and the historical in the writings of the Israeli poet Yehuda Amichai, on the Adamic exuberance of the West Indian Nobel Laureate Derek Walcott, and on the sullen majesty of England's unofficial laureate Philip Larkin. I have followed García Lorca and Joseph Cornell (via Charles Simic) on their forays into New York City and tracked a company of Irish poets, playwrights, and novelists into the Irish countryside, which is for them, as I hope to show, both a real and an imaginary place, a symbol-laden territory. I have included a personal reappraisal of Donald Barthelme's work, which has fallen into a kind of limbo since his death, and I have added a close examination of the biblical story of Jacob's wrestling with an angel from the particular vantage point of the working poet. I have taken the story personally.

For me these pieces reinstate all my hours of wayward, ecstatic reading. Ecstasy is "a state of exalted delight in which normal understanding is felt to be surpassed," and that has often been my own sublime experience of reading. The Greek word *ekstasis* signifies "standing elsewhere" or being "beside oneself," and that, too, is part of my idea of deeply responsive reading, of beyonding. The works I have written about remind me of standing on the shoreline looking out. I feel the rhythm of the waves. I listen to the wind. I think of being called away, called back.

Contents

The Female Yahwist

It takes a leap of readerly imagination for us to consider the actual nature of the archaic Hebrew writer, or writers, who inscribed the oldest stories in what scholars have come to think of as an extremely heterogeneous and composite text: the first five books of the Bible. No one really knows who composed or edited those books—which Jews call the Torah (invariably and somewhat narrowly translated as "Law") or the Pentateuch (which derives from a Greek term meaning "the book of the five scrolls") or the Five Books of Moses—but they have shaped our sensibilities so profoundly that we can scarcely understand how much we are their inventions. No one who grew up reading these biblical stories, so deeply familiar and yet fundamentally strange, or listened to them—as I did—as if history itself were speaking, can ever be entirely free of their influence. The cycle that runs from the creation of Adam to the death of Moses has had an incalculable hold on our imaginations; indeed, what designs these texts have on us, and who in turn designed them, has inspired so much commentary that it could probably be used as landfill for the Dead Sea. Even so, if the literary critic Harold Bloom and the translator David Rosenberg are correct in their audacious work of reconstruction, *The Book of J* (1991), then we have misunderstood some of the most critical dimensions of these narratives. And we have weakly underimagined the author who composed them.

Who is this J that Harold Bloom has called "a vastly eccentric great writer," a genius equal to Dante and Shakespeare, an ironic precursor of Tolstoy, Mann, and Kafka? Previously, J has been considered a documentary source, or sources; a traditional process of accretion, revision, and interpretation; a patchwork

From the *New Yorker*, 21 January 1991. Reprinted with permission.

of laconic narrative passages. Through a long and arduous process, beset by continual disagreements and controversies, biblical scholarship has identified at least five main strands that have come together in the final text of the Pentateuch. J, known as the Yahwist, because of a distinctive use of the name for God (Yahweh or, in German, Jahweh, misspelled as Jehovah), is the most ancient and radically original of these strands. J's text is embedded in the books now called Genesis, Exodus, and Numbers and constitutes the largest single narrative block in the Pentateuch. Most of the great early biblical stories—from the Expulsion to the Exodus—originated with J, perhaps sometime between the mid-tenth and the late ninth century B.C.E. Yet the question of whether or not there ever was an individual J remains open. Hans Schmid, in his book *The Putative Yahwist* (1976), takes the position that the J text developed over a period of four or five hundred years and that, "instead of speaking of the Yahwist as a single collector, author and theologian, one should rather speak of an (inner-) Yahwistic process of editing and interpretation."

There is no consensus on the full dimension of the J text, because the Yahwist was followed by a long succession of other sources, who edited, revised, and, as Bloom would have it, "censored" the original body of stories. After J came E (known as the Elohist, because he refers to God by the plural Elohim, a name that J used for angels), D (the Deuteronomist), and then P, the priestly sources who reworked earlier material and spliced their own didactic interpretations onto it, diluting the combined JE and adding extensive passages of Levitical laws. It is most likely the priestly writers and editors, with their theological, cultic, and institutional concerns, who developed the preliminary canon of the Hebrew Bible. R represents the last stage of the process: the Redactor, or redactors, who selected, changed, and fused all the scrolls together sometime after the Babylonian exile. It was R, conventionally placed in the Academy of Ezra around the year 400 B.C.E.—as much as six hundred years after J—who gave the Torah its decisive formulation.

R was one of the supreme synthesizers of the Hebrew Bible. Critics who have made convincing cases for the literary unity of the Pentateuch—such as Robert Alter, in *The Art of Biblical Narrative* (1981), and Northrop Frye, in *The Great Code* (1982)—are, in effect, praising R's work. As David Damrosch suggests in *The Narrative Covenant* (1987), the later redactors tried to create a text, seamless and whole, that concealed its own compositional history. And what R hoped to obscure approximately twenty-four hundred years ago is precisely what Bloom and Rosenberg have struggled to excavate. Their strategy is to lift the J text from its contextual surroundings in R's Torah and then to translate and interpret it. The result is nothing less than a very old and a very new work of literature, a hypothetical *Book of J*.

In a playful, speculative, and brilliant disquisition on the "Author J" Bloom situates an individual Yahwist in Jerusalem nearly three thousand years ago. He asserts that J was not a professional scribe or copyist, as has sometimes been suggested, even less a court theologian, but, rather, an erudite member of the Solomonic elite who lived at or near the decadent court of King Rehoboam of Judah, Solomon's son and successor (922–915 B.C.E.), and wrote in friendly competition with the Court Historian, the writer responsible for what is now known as 2 Samuel. Bloom's most startling surmise is that J was a woman—a *gevurah*, or "great lady," possibly related to the Court Historian by either blood or marriage, possibly even a princess, one of Solomon's daughters. It is this writer of Davidic royal blood whom Bloom exalts to the highest literary throne, where she somewhat ironically presides, along with Shakespeare, over the spiritual consciousness of Western literature.

Bloom is well aware that his version of the historical J is a fiction, but then, as he suggests, all versions of the early biblical authors—no matter how well grounded in research or attested to by faith—are fictions. Yet his admittedly free speculations are not entirely outside the line of modern biblical scholarship. Like scholars before him, he dismisses the idea of a Mosaic authorship for the Pentateuch as a religious fabrication. As long ago as the twelfth century, Abraham Ibn Ezra circumspectly pointed out that passages in the Torah were inevitably post-Mosaic, and in the seventeenth century Spinoza identified some of the internal discrepancies, divisions, anachronisms, and duplications in the received text, thus inaugurating the "higher" biblical criticism. More recently, such scholars as Gerhard von Rad and Frank Moore Cross have contravened the so-called Documentary Hypothesis (definitively formulated in the nineteenth century) by assuming that there was in actuality only one Yahwist working in the Solomonic period. It was von Rad who first perceived the possible subtext in the J work that connected it to the achievements of the United Monarchy, under David, and to the Solomonic Enlightenment. And it was the late E. A. Speiser, editor of the superb edition of Genesis in the Anchor Bible Series, who deduced a relationship between the Yahwist and the Court Historian. In *King and Kin* (1986) Joel Rosenberg fleshes out the political context of these two possibly companion works, Genesis and 2 Samuel, and in *Who Wrote the Bible?* (1987) Richard Friedman identifies at least six different places where the Yahwist linguistically improvises on the Hebraic root of Rehoboam's name. Mr. Friedman also points out that the J stories are much more sympathetic to women than were later stories by E, and, though he stops short of concluding that J was a woman, he opens up the possibility by suggesting that "we cannot by any means be quick to think of this writer as a man." Bloom relies heavily on this previous scholarship and takes it one step further to assert that J and the Court Historian not only worked together but did so during two distinct periods of history. They share, in his words, "a nostalgia for David, a dubiety about the Solomonic splendor, and an ironic disdain for Rehoboam." The consequences of such a hypothesis are enormous. For example, in this reading of the J text the story of the expulsion from the Garden of Eden becomes less a parable of the Fall, as it has so often been read in Christian revisionism, than a metaphor or trope for the painful transition from Solomon to Rehoboam and the subsequent reduction and dispersal of the kingdom. Many have pointed out that J's work, unlike the revisions of the redactors, is profoundly narrative, earthbound, and humanistic.

Bloom departs from biblical scholarship in his insistence on reading J's work exclusively as a secular text, no more sacred than Tolstoy's novels or Shakespeare's *King Lear*. He disregards oral tradition, declares that distinctions of genre are irrelevant in relation to J's writing, and argues that she was deliberately not creating a national epic. His J was neither a religious nor a historical writer but an aristocratic storyteller. Yet his own critical reading is continually shadowed by the theological aura that surrounds J's greatest literary creation, the character of Yahweh. (No one prays to King Lear.) Indeed, Bloom's boisterous and self-proclaimed antithetical aim is nothing less than to undo a couple of thousand years of institutionalized misreading of J— to cut through the layers of varnish that converted J first into the Torah, then into the Hebrew Bible, and then into the Christian Old Testament. He likes to cite William Blake's maxim that religious history consists of "choosing forms of worship from poetic tales."

Most of the attention that *The Book of J* has thus far received has focused on the polemical contention that J was a woman, a claim that is asserted rather than proved. Part of the argument rests on J's representation of women. For evidence, Bloom suggests that J devoted six times as much space to the creation of woman as to that of man, that she has no heroes but only heroines (Eve, Sarah, Rebecca, Rachel, Tamar, and Zipporah), that human reality is for her domestic and familial rather than royal or priestly, that she undermines and mocks rather than endorses patriarchal authority, and that she exalts women as tougher and more vital than men. This case is intuitively appealing but rationally flawed. From these essentialist arguments one would have to infer, for example, that the creators of *Anna Karenina* and *Madame Bovary* were women.

Bloom has written about J before—most notably in his contribution on Exodus to the book *Congregation* (1987), edited by David Rosenberg, and in the first chapter of his expanded Charles Eliot Norton Lectures at Harvard, *Ruin the Sacred Truths* (1989). The Yahwist also stands as one of his three paradigms for poetic originality in *The Breaking of the Vessels* (1982). In these works Bloom outlined J's quintessential features as a writer of the "Hebraic sublime," but apparently he still considered the Yahwist a male author. As a literary critic, Bloom is well-known for his spirited defense of Romanticism and for his agonistic theory of misreading, which is defined in a tetralogy on literary revisionism—*The Anxiety of Influence* (1973), *A Map of Misreading* (1975), *Kabbalah and Criticism* (1975), and *Poetry and Repression* (1976). He tells us it was in response to feminist critiques of that theory as patriarchal that in the past year he began to develop the notion of a female Yahwist. He was led to it by what he has come to think of as the ironic representation of the biblical patriarchs. In a certain sense the idea of J as a woman serves as a feminist line of defense for his theory of "strong" poets and their aggressive appropriation of literature. No critic has shown a more Nietzschean will to interpretative power over literary texts. He has also resurrected the historical Yahwist with a vengeance against those literary theorists who have proclaimed the so-called death of the author. Perhaps more important, the idea of J as a woman serves as a Bloomian metaphor for the originality he finds in the Yahwistic text. The question of J's sexual identity inevitably points to the issue of J's difference. What is new in J? How does J's Yahweh differ from the god of normative Judaism? Bloom's most engaging idea may be not that J was a woman but that she was essentially a comic writer, a supple and uncanny ironist.

The key to Bloom's conception of J as a Kafkaesque dissembler and a "visionary of incommensurates" hinges on her portrayal of Yahweh. How, he asks, are we to conceive of an all-powerful Yahweh who also haggles with Abram or tries to slay Moses or sits under the trees at Mamre eating veal and curds? Yahweh walks in the garden in the cool of the evening; he shuts Noah's ark himself; he inspects the Tower of Babel. A later proverb such as "The fear of the Lord is the beginning of knowledge" (Proverbs 1:7) seems completely alien to the spirit of J, who shows neither awe nor fear in Yahweh's presence but instead treats him, in Bloom's words, like "an imp who behaves sometimes as though he is rebelling against his Jewish mother, J," and yet he is also God the Father, who makes a sacred covenant with the Jewish people. The Yahweh who is represented as simultaneously human and supreme seems to come from a more archaic tradition of Judaism, now lost to us forever. The heart of the Bloomian argument about the revolutionary originality of J is that the deliberate blasphemy of her work "always was and still is a Yahweh at once human-all-too-human and totally incommensurate with the human." That Blakean Yahweh is exuberant and free of inhibition, willful, possessive, extremely dynamic. At times he operates like the Freudian superego. He is vastly different from the immeasurable, unnamable God of normative Judaism. The writer who dared to imagine that very sly and formidable Creator, Bloom argues, was not a moral theologian but a secular monist, an ironic visionary. But she was first of all a teller of earthly tales.

David Rosenberg's bold new translation of *The Book of J*—

sandwiched between commentaries by Bloom—is especially alert to the abundant wordplay and the elliptical nature of the text. He presents a work that is, in Erich Auerbach's resonant phrase, "fraught with background." His translation allows us to read J apart from the context of the redactors. Rosenberg is not the first to have isolated and reproduced the J text in translation, but his rendition is by far the most literary. He has scrapped the chapter divisions that were retrospectively imposed on the J text and has adopted a sequence of much shorter chapters, which read like multiple scenes from a longer prose work. This structure remains faithful to the gaps and ruptures in the text even as it allows us to consider what remains of the sequence as a whole.

J's text begins not with God's majestic creation of Heaven and earth, which was written by later priestly sources, but in the Judean season of spring when Yahweh scoops up a handful of moistened red clay, shapes it into a human being, and animates it with his own breath. The very name for man (*adam*) is a permanent reminder that human beings come from the earth (*adamah*).

> Before a plant of the field was in earth, before a grain of the field sprouted—Yahweh had not spilled rain on the earth, nor was there man to work the land—yet from the day Yahweh made earth and sky, a mist from within would rise to moisten the surface. Yahweh shaped an earthling from clay of this earth, blew into its nostrils the wind of life. Now look: man becomes a creature of flesh.

Yahweh plants a garden in Eden, molds the clay into "all the creatures of the field and birds of the air," and brings them to man curious to see what he will name them. This is the beginning of human language, the primal act of poetic creation. But man still lacks an equivalent being, and so Yahweh puts him into a deep sleep and then takes one of his ribs and shapes or builds it into a nameless woman, the first living being forged not from earth but from another living being. This is what Keats called Adam's dream, comparable to the Imagination: "He awoke and found it truth." The Hebrew word for *man, ish* (used in the sense of an individual being, as opposed to the word *adam*, which is generic and undifferentiated), appears here, connecting him permanently to woman, *isha*. Bloom's commentary on the creation of a second sex is especially amusing: "Surely J's ironic point is that the second time around, Yahweh has learned better how the job ought to be done."

Rosenberg's translation of the next passage suggests that man is both consoled and haunted by a sense of lost unity and wholeness with the woman, whom he later names Eve, or Hava (*hawa*).

"This one is bone of my bone, flesh of my flesh," said the man. "Woman I call her, out of man she was parted." So a man parts from his mother and father, clings to his wife: they were one flesh.

What follows is the story that has had such a scandalous history in our culture—the tale of Adam and Eve and the serpent. J's version reads less like a theological parable of temptation, sin, guilt, and punishment—in other words, less like the Christian Fall—than like the story of an aggrieved parent and his offending children. It enacts what Bloom calls their "wounding estrangement" from God, playing out a painful family triangle and romance.

After the Expulsion come the stories of Cain and Abel, the Race of Giants, Noah and the Flood, the Tower of Babel. We enter into the sweep of patriarchal history with the Call of Abram out of his homeland and the promise to him of "greatness, a nation and a blessing." This blessing, the call for more life, inaugurates the cycle of Abram and Sarah. Here are J's spare unforgettable versions of the cutting of a sacred covenant between Yahweh and Abram; of Yahweh's appearance to Abram among the oaks of Mamre; of the destruction of Sodom and Gomorrah and the crystallization of Lot's wife into salt; of Isaac and Rebecca and the long, internecine rivalry of their twin sons; of Jacob's marriage to Rachel and of his nightlong struggle with a mysterious stranger who turns out to be a divine being who both injures him and renames him Israel, in a place that he, in turn, renames Deiface ("I've seen God face to face, yet my flesh holds on"). The second half of the J text tells the extended saga of Joseph (whom Bloom reads as J's surrogate for her revered David), of Pharaoh, of Moses and the Exodus—Israel freed from Egyptian hands, and four decades of wandering in the wilderness, until the blessing is fulfilled, until the making of a binding covenant between Moses and Yahweh on Mt. Sinai. It tells the droll story of Balaam and concludes with Moses' vision of the Promised Land ("It is revealed to your eyes, though your body cannot follow") and his death and then his burial in an unknown grave.

Anyone who has tried to translate even a small portion of the Pentateuch knows how difficult the task can be. One has to contend with classical Hebrew, with thousands and thousands of pages of religious commentary and biblical scholarship, with a heavily revised and bowdlerized text, with the majestic splendors of the King James Bible, or Authorized Version (1611), which has set the standard for English prose since the seventeenth century. "That old tongue with its clang and its flavor," Edmund Wilson said. "We have been living with it all our lives." There is also the modern competition of the Revised Standard Version (1952); the Jerusalem Bible, which is Catholic (1966); the New English Bible, which is Protestant (1970); and the New American Jewish Version (1982). Of course, in all those translations J is effaced and incorporated into the larger rhythms of the Hebrew Bible.

Rosenberg's innovative translation struggles to re-create J's distinctive voice, a tone of modulated ironic grandeur. His version is replete with self-conscious puns, verbal pyrotechnics, and elaborate repetitions, words echoing within words. Dazzling as it is, this idiom can seem forced and unnecessarily convoluted, as in chapter 6, when Yahweh questions Adam:

> "Who told you naked is what you are?" he asked. "Did you touch the tree I desired you not eat?"

Certainly, we think, Yahweh could have learned to speak English more naturally than this. And it's hard to know what to make of Esau's complaint to his father:

> "Was he named Jacob, heel-clutcher . . . that he might jaywalk behind me, twice?"

These anachronisms and verbal contortions create a literary text that is at times unusually difficult to read.

Rosenberg follows J in continually shifting between past and present tenses. He also reproduces what seem in the Hebrew to be purposely ambiguous pronouns, which often make it difficult to distinguish who is speaking. What was translated as *and* and *behold* in older versions, and as *when, if, then,* etc., in more recent versions, he has rendered as *now* or *now listen* or *now look* or *watch* or *so it was,* depending on the context. This creates a sense of genuine directness but also a jumpy, offbeat rhythm, a music that is filled with jolts and jump-starts—*The Book of J* rendered in the fractured idiom of John Berryman's "Homage to Mistress Brad-street" or *77 Dream Songs.* Ezra Pound's description of William Carlos Williams's characteristic "volts, jerks, sulks, balks, out-blurts and jump-overs" sounds a bit like the language of Rosen-berg's J. And, just as in Berryman and Williams, the American version of J can have a surprising offhanded eloquence, as in:

> Now Abimelech proclaimed for all: "One who touches this man and his wife has felt his own death."

Or:

> They moved on from Sukkot, marked out their camp at Eitam, at the border of the desert. Yehweh walks ahead of them each day in a pillar of cloud, marking the way: at night, in a pillar of fire. Day or night, the people can walk. Ahead of them, it never disap-pears: a pillar of fire by night, a pillar of cloud by day.

In these passages it is possible to detect the splendors of the writer that Bloom and Rosenberg have constructed for us.

After reading *The Book of J,* one can never consider the oldest strand in the Hebrew Bible in quite the same way as before. J seems as poignantly real and fictive a figure as Homer or Shakespeare or the Court Historian, who was supposedly her friend. She is an elusive presence; indeed, we are not convinced that she ever existed, and yet we become collabora-tors in imagining her. There is a Midrash on Psalms that says the Torah was written "in black fire upon white fire." I think of the author who inscribed those flames. She is using the Phoeni-cian–Old Hebrew script and writing on papyrus with a reed pen in one of Rehoboam's courtyards. Or maybe she is carving words into a leather scroll with a dull knife. With what political nostalgia does she daydream about the days of King David? With what fierce joy does she imagine Yahweh walking through a grove of trees or moving across the desert at night in a pillar of fire? With what tragic sense of wonder does she write:

> And look: they are naked, man and woman, untouched by shame, not knowing it.

A Fresh Hell

The journey into the underworld is one of the most obsessively recurring stories of the Western imagination. Something in us thrills to the metaphor of a hero descending into the bowels of the earth, into the region of demons and lost souls, and escaping to tell the tale. Greek mythology is filled with such fabulous descents: a Thracian minstrel (Orpheus) sings so poignantly that he charms his way into the netherworld to reclaim his lost bride; a man of murderous physical prowess (Hercules) sets off for Hades to retrieve a hellhound with three heads and a snake's tail in order to fulfill the last of twelve labors. In book 11 of Homer's Odyssey, Odysseus sails his ship into a country where the sun never shines, and there, pouring libations to the dead, he summons a swarm of ghosts, among them an unburied friend, his aged mother, and the seer Tiresias. This is echoed in book 6 of Virgil's Aeneid, when Aeneas persuades the Sibyl of Cumae to guide him into Hades, so he can speak with his dead father about the future. As Homer's scene informed Virgil's, so Virgil's account served as a prototype for Dante's *Inferno*—the most entrancing, detailed, and audacious treatment of a human being's journey into Hell ever written.

The Divine Comedy consists of a hundred cantos, divided into three parts: *Inferno, Purgatorio,* and *Paradiso.* It is at once a metaphysical adventure story (a pilgrim goes forth to discover the fate of souls after death), a personal odyssey understood in allegorical terms ("Midway on our life's journey," the poem famously begins, "I found myself / In dark woods"), an encyclopedic guide to the schematics of the otherworld (from the doomed in Hell through the atoning sinners in Purgatory to the blessed souls in Heaven), and a quest beyond the grave for a visionary beauty (Beatrice,

From the *New Yorker*, 23 January 1995. Reprinted with permission.

who is at different times compared to divine grace in the church, to the Virgin Mary, and even to Christ himself). The poem is a kind of Augustinian confession: a search for the Absolute written under the sign of eternity, a conversion narrative about losing one's way and turning toward God's light. The *Inferno* is the first installment of the pilgrim's three-part spiritual journey, but it seems to have held a nearly exclusive claim on the majority of modern readers. James Merrill has pointed out that "to most twentieth-century readers the *Inferno is* Dante." Apparently, the siren song of damnation calls to us in ways that atonement and salvation do not—perhaps because we recognize ourselves in the lost, unhappy sinners who emanate from the shadows.

In guiding us through a permanently apocalyptic landscape, Dante was also representing his idea of life on earth. In the foreword to Robert Pinsky's splendid translation, *The Inferno of Dante* (1995), John Freccero, the dean of American Dante scholars, notes, "Hell is the state of the soul after death, but it is also the state of the world as seen by an exile whose experience has taught him no longer to trust the world's values." Dante was exiled in perpetuity from his beloved city of Florence on false political charges in 1302, and by the time he wrote the *Inferno*—the poem is set in 1300 but was composed sometime between 1307 and 1314—he had come to view his birthplace with the skeptical, unforgiving eye of a disabused lover. Here is the opening salvo of canto 26:

> Rejoice, O Florence, since you are so great,
> Beating your wings on land and on the sea,
> That in Hell too your name is spread about!
>
> I found among those there for their thievery
> Five of your citizens . . .

So the *Inferno* is, among other things, a fantastic dream of retribution, "a pawnshop in which all the countries and cities known to Dante were left unredeemed" (Osip Mandelstam), and a treatise on the corrupt and degraded state of society. We don't share Dante's medieval cosmology or politics, but twentieth-century readers have had no trouble recognizing his portrait of Hell as a stand-in for a secular human city.

The Inferno of Dante is an informative bilingual edition, with the Italian printed *en face*. It has Freccero's excellent foreword; useful notes; a detailed plan of Dante's journey through Hell; and thirty-five black-and-white monotypes by the artist Michael Mazur. These are beautifully eerie and restrained—a visual backdrop to the dark night of the soul that constitutes Dante's voyage. Most important, Robert Pinsky's verse translation is fast-paced, idiomatic, and accurate. It moves with the concentrated gait of a lyric poem—the *Inferno* is, after all, an account of two poets, Dante and his guide, Virgil, walking through the nine descending circles of Hell—and the grand sweep of a nineteenth-century novel: Hell is filled with Dostoyevskian sufferers, disenfranchised crowds, Sadean torments. The primary strength of this translation is the way it maintains the original's episodic and narrative velocity while mirroring its formal shape and character. It is no small achievement to reproduce Dante's rhyme scheme and at the same time sound fresh and natural in English, and Pinsky succeeds in creating a supple American equivalent for Dante's vernacular music where many others have failed. This translator is first and foremost a poet.

Dante wrote the *Commedia* in Italian, which in his day was still a nebulous national language, rather than in the customary literary language of Latin, in order to be accessible to a wider audience. He compares himself to David, the "humble psalmist," and, in a sense, his poem sets itself up as a colloquial rival to Scripture. It claims enormous truths for itself in a fresh style. The language is by turns stately, demotic, and mercurial. It can be scholastically dense or intimately conversational. Neologisms, regional dialects, and Latin borrowings abound. Didactic stretches accelerate into passages of dizzying verbal majesty as souls become corporeal and words metamorphose into things. There is no replicating this linguistic richness in another language. As the Italian axiom has it, "Traduttore traditore" (The translator is a traitor), and in truth the back stacks of our libraries are littered with treacheries, but Pinsky takes his place in a line of estimable poetic predecessors—among them Henry Wadsworth Longfellow (1867) and Laurence Binyon (1933)— who have not only wrestled with Dante's content but also found adventurous formal equivalents for his style and music.

Dante's use of terza rima, a marvelous instrument that he devised specifically for the *Commedia,* is the greatest obstacle to translating the poem into English. He composed his poem in interlocking three-line stanzas called *terzine*, or tercets, which rhyme in the pattern *aba, bcb, cdc*, etc. Rhyming the first and third lines gives each tercet a sense of temporary closure; rhyming the second line with the first and last lines of the next stanza generates a strong feeling of propulsion. The effect is both open-ended and conclusive, like moving through a series of interpenetrating rooms (indeed, the Italian word *stanza* means "room") or going down a set of winding stairs: you are always traveling forward while looking backward. The movement is reinforced by Dante's skillful use of the hendecasyllabic (eleven-syllable) line common to Italian poetry. Its rhythm incarnates the spiraling action of the form; in fact, many scholars have pointed to the spiral as the closest geometric equivalent to terza rima. (One has even compared it to the helixes of DNA.) The momentum of each canto—an urgency slowed by retrospection—mirrors the larger voyage of the pilgrim through the poem.

It has been estimated that translating the entire *Divine Comedy* into terza rima requires more than forty-five hundred triple rhymes in English. This is a staggering number; whereas Italian is abundantly rich in rhyme, English is relatively poor. English rhymes are also more emphatic than Italian ones, more ringing and noticeable. No wonder that Byron labeled Dante "the most untranslatable of poets." Previous translations have often buckled under the nearly intolerable weight of trying to reproduce Dante's form in credible English. Even such ambitious formal versions of the *Inferno* as those by Dorothy Sayers (1949) and John Ciardi (1954)—who uses a "dummy," or defective, terza rima, leaving out the linking middle rhyme—contort English syntax and strain English diction in order to match the Italian rhyme scheme. It's easy for the imitator of terza rima to feel, in the English poet C. H. Sisson's phrase, "like a clown following a ballet dancer," and in recent decades the most accurate translations have tended to shun rhyme altogether.

The student of the *Inferno* can turn with confidence to the prose version of the Dante scholar Charles Singleton (1970), the most comprehensive annotated edition in our language, and to the blank-verse versions of Mark Musa (1971), Sisson himself (1980), Allen Mandelbaum (1980), and Tom Phillips (1985), whose jaunty carriage makes his blank verse especially pleasurable. These versions gesture toward the poem's form—its body—without trying to approximate its true shape. Even Longfellow, whose translation is a magnificent work in its own right, eschews rhyme in favor of a Miltonic blank verse. Every translator knows that terza rima isn't extraneous to Dante's work (T. S. Eliot once said that "Dante *thought* in terza rima"), but that doesn't make it any less difficult to transport. As if to make the point, Shelley's "Triumph of Life," the finest English poem ever written in the form, was unfinished at his death.

There have been at least fifty renderings of the *Inferno* into English in our century, but Pinsky's is the first rhyming translation unmarred by antiquarianism. He consistently employs slant or half-rhymes (*pain/sin/down; night/thought/it*) as well as full rhymes (*dwell/Hell/well*), in order to re-create Dante's form while remaining true to his meaning. Consonantal rhyming, based on similar rather than identical internal vowel sounds, allows for a more flexible, more complex, and more dissonant sense of rhythm and harmony. This tactic is crucial when it comes to rhyming disyllabic words, since triple half-rhymes (*quiet/spirit/merit*) don't stop with the dull thud that triple full rhymes do (*quailing/railing/wailing*) at the ends of English lines. It is precisely these disyllabic, or "feminine," rhymes that have undone so many previous translators. Pinsky's use of Dickinson's or Yeats's method of slant rhyme—to name only two of the poets who fully mastered its effects—supplied him with, in his words, "an audible scaffold of English terza rima, a scaffold that does not distort the English sentence, or draw excessively on the reaches of the English lexicon."

Pinsky also makes accommodations and compromises. He readily admits that he doesn't follow the original line by line, or even stanza by stanza, and that at times he foreshortens cantos in order to mimic Dante's epigrammatic compression. Occasionally, Pinsky, too, wrenches rhymes into place; it's hard to imagine anyone actually saying, "Although their burden held them in retard" (23) or "which wins all battles if it does not despond" (24). While Pinsky uses enjambment—the carrying of phrases across lines—as one of his most successful strategies, he moves sentences across both lines and stanzas more aggressively than Dante and so runs the risk of emphasizing the poem's forward momentum at the expense of its retrospective vistas. Yet this tactic also enables him to capture the poem's swirling downward rhythm—what Dante calls "the hurricane of Hell in perpetual motion."

Dante's verse has a depth and gravity—at times whirling and tumultuous, at times stately and processional—that Pinsky captures exceedingly well. Here is how he translates the traditional epic invocation that begins canto 2:

> Day was departing, and the darkening air
> Called all earth's creatures to their evening quiet
> While I alone was preparing as though for war
>
> To struggle with my journey and with the spirit
> Of pity, which flawless memory will redraw:
> O Muses, O genius of art, O memory whose merit
>
> Has inscribed inwardly those things I saw—
> Help me fulfill the perfection of your nature.

These well-modulated lines evoke Dante's dark misgivings at the beginning of his project, his sense of foreboding as he battles exhaustion and despair. The pilgrim is about to descend into the underworld—"I am no Aeneas or Paul," he will soon declare—and wonders whether he is capable of sustaining a journey beyond death. He knows he will struggle with misplaced sympathy for the damned. And he questions whether he is worthy enough to write the epic (a contemporary Bible? a new Aeneid?) that we are about to read. Thus the triple invocation to the Muses, to the presiding spirit of art, and to the interior god of memory.

To appreciate the cadenced grandeur and Virgilian echoes of Pinsky's flexible iambic pentameter, one has only to compare it to a stilted rendering such as that by Dorothy Sayers: "Day was departing and the dusk drew on, / Loosing from labour every living thing / Save me, in all the world; I—I alone— / Must gird me to the wars—rough travelling." Sayers is actually a stricter translator than Pinsky. She follows Dante's lines and line endings more closely than he does, but one practically has to translate her translation ("I—I alone— / Must gird me to the wars"?) in order to figure out what the poet is saying. She distorts the syntax to maintain the rhymes, in the process making Dante sound like a weak Victorian poet.

A prose crib such as Charles Singleton's, which is nothing if not literal, seems to stand at the opposite extreme from Sayers's high-sounding verse. Here is his rendering of the same passage:

> Day was departing, and the dark air was taking the creatures on earth from their labors; and I alone was making ready to sustain the strife, both of the journey and of the pity, which unerring memory shall retrace. O Muses, O high genius, help me now! O memory that wrote down what I saw, here shall your worthiness appear!

This is preferable to Sayers, because, if nothing else, it's more accurate, and yet poetic models have to come from somewhere, even if they are outmoded or absorbed and expressed unconsciously. Singleton's intentionally flat version starts off agreeably enough, but soon he, too, imitates an archaic diction—"and I alone was making ready to sustain the strife"—that is alien to contemporary speech. And the phrase "both of the journey and of the pity," while it is an exact translation from the Italian, doesn't say much in English. What does it mean to "sustain the strife . . . of the pity"? The translator who is too much a literalist—even such a great Dantista as Singleton—runs the risk of transposing the words but sacrificing their meaning.

Pinsky steers a sure course between the Scylla and Charybdis of dogged literalism and high-flown lyricism, and as a result the contemporary reader experiences the startling seriousness of a pilgrimage that begins in dark woods, falters in the vestibule of Hell, and then proceeds according to an exact route from Limbo and the upper regions toward the center point of the earth. Dante takes pains to describe the journey with geometric and astrological precision, and Mazur has provided an "aerial view" with a schematic overlay at the beginning of canto 11.

The protagonist of Dante's poem is bewildered by both what he sees and what he doesn't see in the shadowy nether regions, and he repeatedly turns to Virgil for explanations. Here, in Pinsky's strong mimetic rendering, is his initial encounter with the abyss:

> The sighs, groans and laments at first were so loud,
> Resounding through starless air, I began to weep:
> Strange languages, horrible screams, words imbued

With rage or despair, cries as of troubled sleep
Or of a tortured shrillness—they rose in a coil
Of tumult, along with noises like the slap

Of beating hands, all fused in a ceaseless flail
That churns and frenzies that dark and timeless air
Like sand in a whirlwind. And I, my head in a swirl

Or error, cried: "Master, what is this I hear?"

In a spirited tale of mentorship Virgil glosses the sights and
sounds of Hell and leads Dante through its physical and spiri-
tual geography. The pilgrim is overwhelmed by the number of
wretched souls passing before his eyes. One inevitably thinks of
The Waste Land at the lines "I would not have thought / Death
had undone so many," and, in fact, Eliot's work captures better
than most the Dantesque world of living ghosts—the terrifying
isolation of souls unmoored from community, alienated even
from themselves. At every stage Dante encounters individuals
who want to tell him their heartbreaking stories: Francesca of
Rimini, Ulysses, Count Ugolino, and a host of others. This is a
key social aspect of the poem, which makes it feel both contem-
porary and historically rich.

In Dante's underworld every figure stands for his own trans-
gression. Dante borrowed from Aquinas the Aristotelian term
contrapasso, or law of retribution, to designate a system in which
the punishment distills and matches the crime. Sin is liter-
alized: those who succumbed to anger tear perpetually at one
another's naked bodies; gluttons wallow in putrid soil and get
chewed by Cerberus; murderers boil in a river of blood. In an
insightful note Pinsky suggests that Dante's portrayal of the
living dead anticipates the Romantic creation of horror as a
literary—and, later, cinematic—genre. The uncanny metamor-
phosis of human beings continues to intensify throughout the
poem, since the farther down Dante and Virgil go the more
heinous are the crimes they encounter, until finally, in the
darkness of point zero, they crawl across the body of Lucifer
himself.

At the conclusion of the poem the pilgrim (and, by exten-
sion, the reader) feels a liberating sense of release at escaping
Hell and glimpsing the heavens again:

To get back up to the shining world from there
My guide and I went into that hidden tunnel:

And following its path, we took no care
To rest, but climbed: he first, then I—so far,
Through a round aperture I saw appear

Some of the beautiful things that Heaven bears,
Where we came forth, and once more saw the stars.

In recent times it has been argued, by Erich Auerbach, among others, that Dante's characters are so sympathetically drawn and so realistically portrayed that they subvert the rigid categories in which the allegorist has ensnared them. Dante's medieval typology (the progression from Sins of Incontinence to Sins of Fraud) doesn't mean much to us anymore. It is not the "allegory of theologians" but the flawed humanity of Dante's characters that excites and touches readers. In Auerbach's words, "the beyond becomes a stage for human beings and human passions." This is a tempting argument. It's not particularly troubling to think of schismatics being divided from themselves, but it's another matter to encounter the Provençal poet Bertran de Born, who was beheaded, and whose trunk is forever carrying around his severed head, "gripping its hair like a lantern, letting it swing." And while it's one thing to learn of political treachery that send traitors to Antenora, in the ninth circle, it's quite another to witness Ugolino, who died of starvation, gnawing his enemy's skull and reliving the story of his gruesome last days. The suffering of individuals writhing in the torture cell of eternity calls out to us from beyond the grave.

Yet in any full reading of the *Inferno* it is crucial to distinguish between two Dantes: the pilgrim passing through the divisions and subdivisions of Hell and the poet "remembering" the journey and writing an epic poem about it. Readers identify with the pilgrim, whose heart goes out to "the disconsolate and mutilated shades," but that pilgrim can be readily distinguished from the author, who is unwavering in his judgments. For example, as Freccero notes, the pilgrim Dante seems truly anguished to discover his mentor Brunetto Latini among the sodomites in the seventh circle, but it must be remembered that the poet Dante placed him there. God didn't write the *Inferno* or decide that there would be no reprieves in the City of Woes or inscribe over the portals the infamous words "Abandon All Hope, You Who Enter Here." Freccero puts the matter succinctly: "In spite of Dante's reputation as the greatest of Christian poets, there is no sign of Christian forgiveness in the 'Inferno.' The dominant theme is not mercy but justice, dispensed with the severity of the ancient law of retribution." Readers will always find that the humane perspective of the pilgrim clashes with the viewpoint of the icy administrator of justice, and that's precisely the point. The tension between the temporal and the transcendental orders—between guilty individuals crying out and an anonymous system of justice relentlessly dispensing with them—is what gives the poem so much of its terrifying force and the poet his complex, judicial grandeur.

Pinsky's translation is well suited to our time. He has created an idiom that brilliantly suggests the work of both a medieval allegorist and a protomodern thinker and, above all, of a writer—one who dramatizes the desperate vulnerability of human beings caught up in an implacable world. At our own apocalyptic moment in history the reader can scarcely forget that the *Inferno* is a book in which the earth opens and the historical world is suspended outside time. The progress of the soul through the underworld is a theme that cannot date, but it does seem to have special relevance to the modern dilemma. Perhaps that's why the *Inferno,* as opposed to the *Purgatorio* and the *Paradiso,* has inspired so many devastating modern works, which burn with a true infernal flame—from Gogol's *Dead Souls* and Conrad's *Heart of Darkness* to Eliot's *Waste Land,* Camus's *The Fall,* and Malcolm Lowry's *Under the Volcano.* Dante seems to have anticipated the nervous, unholy epoch in which we find ourselves. Purgatory and Paradise belong to the ages, but Hell is recognizably ours.

Emerson

"Life is an Ecstasy"

"I never was on a coach that went fast enough for me," Ralph Waldo Emerson once confessed, and, indeed, there is a wild, nervy, nearly out-of-control quality to his best writing. He was a passionate intellectual explorer setting forth for the unknown and flinging himself into the wilderness of experience. His essays are a clarion call for movement, action, transport. Emerson's idea of writing was to fire all his arrows and then throw his own body at the target. He held nothing back. One of his keywords was *contact;* another was *abandonment.* He abhorred stasis and could never rest or stay still for long. "Power ceases in the instant of repose," he wrote in his manifesto "Self-Reliance." "It resides in the movement of transition from a past to a new state, in the shooting of the gulf, in the darting to an aim." He was a remarkably fluid thinker, a philosopher of "fluxions and mobility" who asserted that "everything good is on the highway." He liked to step on the accelerator and storm past crossings and thresholds into new territory, new ideas. One of our most volatile and vehicular writers, he can also seem maddeningly elusive. Try to pin him down, and he surges away, turning up elsewhere. "Every thing teaches transition, transference, metamorphosis: therein is human power," he declared in his journals. "We dive & reappear in new places."

Emerson's passionate nature has often been underestimated. "Do your thing, and I shall know you," the philosopher said (later he revised it to "Do your work, and I shall know you"), yet

---

Originally appeared as "The Red-Hot Transcendentalist," *New Yorker,* 10 July 1995. Reprinted with permission.

it has proved especially difficult to bring together his inner and outer lives. Who was this unsettled and unsettling thinker who said, "A foolish consistency is the hobgoblin of little minds"? It's as unproductive to deify him as a plaster sage or "some new kind of saint—perhaps Unitarian" (W. C. Brownell) as to condescend to him as a "champion of cheerfulness" (George Santayana). Despite difficulties, admirable biographical efforts have been made in the past—by Ralph L. Rusk (1949), Gay Wilson Allen (1981), and John McAleer (1984), among others—but Robert D. Richardson Jr.'s splendid *Emerson: The Mind on Fire* (1995) is the first biography that locates the source of Emerson's volcanic power in his emotional depth and searing intellectual intensity. "Emerson really had passion; he wrote it," Gertrude Stein perceived, and Richardson presses home the point by exploring this side of Emerson's character. The result is a suggestive and sympathetic work that gets to the heart of the man who felt that "life is an ecstasy."

The clue to Emerson's character may well lie in his need to keep growing at all costs and his unappeasable hunger for first-hand experience. Richardson has a healthy regard for the elusiveness of his subject and sets out to reconstruct the "natural history" of Emerson's enthusiasms. He states that his book began as a companion to his intellectual biography of Henry Thoreau (1986) but that, because Emerson's intellectual development proved inextricable from his personal and social experiences, it turned into a full-scale biography. He thus takes to heart Emerson's first lesson—that everything emerges from the emergent self. We measure a man by his angle to the universe, Emerson claims. History is grounded in biography, and transcendental philosophy is anchored in individual experience. To understand Emerson, it is necessary to puncture the aura of deadly sobriety that still clings to him. He was Dionysian at heart. "Freed of his vast, unfortunate, and self-perpetuating reputation," Richardson writes, "Emerson steps forth as a complicated, energetic, and emotionally intense man who habitually spoke against the status quo and in favor of whatever was wild and free." He was a prism of contending forces—an extravagant thinker and fiery individualist who was also, in Richardson's words, "a good neighbor, an activist citizen, a fond father, a loyal brother, and a man whose many friendships framed his life." The sense that the biographer actually likes his subject pervades this account of Emerson's life.

The book is divided into a shapely hundred chapters: a collection of four- to seven-page essays—each revolving around some aspect of Emerson's life or thought—deftly organized into chronological sequence. A historical timetable operates in the background. Time and again, Richardson proves that Emerson, an embracer at heart, had deep reserves of skepticism. Consequently, the biography begins not with one of the fabled affirmations but with a critical moment when its subject was twenty-eight years old. Already ministering to a prominent Boston church, Emerson was in the midst of a vocational crisis, questioning the sacrament of Communion and the idea of Christian immortality. His twenty-year-old wife, Ellen, whom he adored, had died fourteen months before, and he habitually walked out to the cemetery where she was buried. On March 29, 1832, he did something unusual, something he would repeat after his five-year-old son died: he opened the coffin and peered in. Richardson treats the first of these episodes as an emblematic act of confrontation, satisfying Emerson's craving for "direct, personal, unmediated experience." Maybe it was also his way of letting Ellen go. By year's end he had resigned his ministry and sailed for Europe. It is crucial to recall Emerson as, among other things, a bereft widower and failed minister, repeatedly struggling with his own griefs and doubts in order to become a foursquare affirmer.

Born in 1803, he was the third of six sons (he also had two sisters, both of whom died in early childhood), and he was generally considered the least promising of the bunch. He was the silly kid in the family and the overlooked one. Years later, he asserted, "the advantage in education is always with those children who slip up into life without being objects of notice." The most striking figure of his youth was his father's sister, Mary Moody Emerson. This eccentric maiden aunt has often been caricatured and mined for good anecdotes (for starters, she was four feet three inches tall and slept in a coffin-shaped bed), but Richardson correctly views her as the single most important influence on her nephew Ralph's intellectual development, as a formidably outspoken and energetic religious thinker, an American Jakob Böhme. Emerson deemed his Aunt Mary "the best writer in Massachusetts." He copied out her letters and recorded her conversations in a manuscript that totaled eight hundred and seventy pages. Her unpublished writings were one of his main sourcebooks. Unlike his father, a nonreligious Unitarian, his aunt was a "deistic pietist," an exuberant visionary who saw death as life's culminating experience. Her motto was "Always do what you are afraid to do." She came to disapprove of her nephew's ideas, but more than anyone else she inspired him to think for himself.

A basic mystery of Emerson's life is how a mediocre college student and seemingly conventional young man turned himself into a bold, iconoclastic proponent of freedom and self-reliance. Sometime during his junior year at Harvard, his sense of himself changed. He stopped calling himself Ralph and started using the Waldo. He began writing poetry seriously, kept a list of everything he read, and entitled a series of notebooks "Wide World." Something had lit up from within, and he spent his days "reading and writing and talking and walking." He loved religious eloquence—enthusiasm was his natural habitat—and soon was on the path to becoming a poet, an essayist, an orator.

Emerson was an avid, creative, and intoxicated reader, and his reading was continuously available to him because of his assiduous journal keeping. He jotted down quotations, summarized arguments, appended comments on what he read. He registered everything personally, treating it as grist for his own testamentary writing. He said, "The student is to read history actively and not passively; to esteem his own life the text, and books the commentary."

He combed thousands of volumes searching for what he called "lustres," and his biography is in good measure the story of a man who read in order to think and feel and who often treated literature as a stimulus for ecstasy. He devoured memoirs, travel books, and religious autobiography as well as poetry. (He wrote: "I am born a poet, of a low class without doubt yet a poet. This is my nature and vocation.") Richardson shows him struggling to overcome Hume's skepticism, embracing Montaigne and Goethe, reading Plato through "at least seven discernible stages." He illustrates how enthusiastically Emerson responded to natural history and astronomy, how transcendentalism grew from his reading of Wordsworth, Coleridge, and Carlyle, how he internalized Hebrew and Christian classics and resonated to the mystical writing of Pythagoras and Plotinus, Swedenborg and Böhme, venturing out to the religious literatures of Persia, India, and China. Reading enlarged him, but from the start he came to everything as an equal unwilling to defer or yield. He read in order to put reading aside. As Lewis Mumford wrote, "With most of the resources of the past at his command, Emerson achieved nakedness."

Writing things down was Emerson's way of thinking about them. The journals, really an assortment of notebooks, ledgers, and diaries, amount to more than three million words and some two hundred and sixty-three volumes of observations, anecdotes, conversations, ideas, meditations, dreams, and epiphanies. They are a stupendous work in and of themselves, and no selection could ever do them full justice. Not only do they contain Emerson's most genuine writing; they also turn a searchlight on nineteenth-century literature and life.

The journals reveal Emerson in all moods—cheerful, sarcastic, disoriented, panicky, self-critical, resolute, oracular. They show the intensity of his crises, the setbacks to his quest for self-realization, the recuperative force of his mind. They show how deeply he dreamed of being an Adamic, or primal, man. Here, for example, is an entry from the 1840s:

> I dreamed that I floated at will in the great Ether, and I saw this world floating also not far off, but diminished to the size of an apple. Then an angel took it in his hand and brought it to me and said, "This must thou eat." And I ate the world.

Nearly all Emerson's great ideas came to him first as journal entries. He called the journals his "savings bank" and used them to construct his lectures and essays. His method—moving from unguarded diary entries and personal reflections to generalized statements and completed essays—illustrates how painstakingly he worked. Organization of argument was never his strength, and it's evident how desperately he struggled with language as a medium. "Here I sit and read and write with very little system, and as far as regards composition, with the most fragmentary results; paragraphs incompressible, each sentence an infinitely repellent particle." Reading the journals, we see how deeply he oscillated between rhapsody and despair, his heady self-confidence undermined by an involuntary nihilism. The journals additionally clarify why he called himself "a rocket manufacturer." His majestic sentences tend to break loose from their context and stand alone as aphorisms.

"I do then with my friends as I do with my books," Emerson wrote in his essay "Friendship," thus disclosing a complex truth about himself. He both welcomed and resisted his many friends. He worked tirelessly on their behalf but also viewed them across an unbridgeable gulf of solitude. His massive interiority was at odds with his cool visage. He burned internally and reproved himself for "superficial coldness and prudence." Yet his Yankee exterior served as protective coloration. He was determined to reach the heights and the depths on his own. "I am God in nature," he declared. "I am a weed by the wall." He radiated well-being from the lectern, but he referred to himself in writing as the "sad, estranged, misadventured, estrayed Waldo Emerson" and confided that after the age of thirty a man wakes up sad virtually every morning. Each of his excruciating personal losses—his wife Ellen (1831), his brother Charles (1836), and his son Waldo (1842)—left him unstrung and directionless, debilitated by grief yet ultimately strengthened in his commitment to self-reliance and resolved to move on. He believed in the law of compensation and the transfer of energy: countering sadness with enthusiasm, ennui with work, isolation with colloquy. Process was all.

Emerson was especially responsive to quirky and grand visionaries. He was drawn to Jones Very, a self-styled "new born bard of the Holy Ghost," and to the shouting Methodist Edward Taylor. ("It may be that Emerson is going to hell," Taylor said, "but . . . he will change the climate there, and emigration will set that way.") He made deep connections with Thomas Carlyle and that most difficult disciple Henry Thoreau. And he responded brilliantly to the democratic cosmos of Walt Whitman. "I am not blind to the worth of the wonderful gift of *Leaves of Grass*," he wrote in what has become the most well-known letter in American literature. "I find it the most extraordinary piece of wit and wisdom that America has yet contributed." Whitman, for his part, understood that for American writers Emerson could never be wholly rejected. "Even when he falls on stony ground," Whitman said, "he somehow eventuates in a harvest."

It's hard to get an exact fix on Emerson's second marriage, to Lydia Jackson, in 1835, the most important relationship of his middle age. Their reserve was daunting. She always called him Mr. Emerson. Their daughter Ellen said, "The tremendous manner in which she loved father was always as astonishing to me as the coolness with which she treated him." More clear-cut, though still cloudy, was Emerson's friendship with Margaret Fuller. For a ten-year period, beginning in 1836, they regarded each other as something like soul mates. "I shall never go quite back to my old arctic habits," he wrote her, yet she complained that he held himself back. Fuller also introduced him to the free-spirited Caroline Sturgis, to whom he was warmly attracted. Is it too much to suggest, as Richardson does, that "in the early 1840s Emerson was living emotionally, though not physically, in what would now be called an open marriage"? No one knows whom, if anyone, Emerson was thinking of in his full-blown celebration of eros: "The heart has its Sabbath and jubilees in which the world appears as a hymeneal feast, and the natural sounds and the circle of the seasons are erotic odes and dances."

Richardson follows Emerson's professional life from his abandoned ministry to his fame as a public intellectual. He covers all Emerson's key lectures, surveys his major books, examines his editorship of the *Dial*, traces his progress as a religious thinker and a proponent of American cultural ideals. And he eagerly shows Emerson responding as a social radical to current events. ("If a soul be taken and crushed by democracy till it utter a cry, that cry will be Emerson," John Jay Chapman wrote.) He was a party of one whose platform was "the infinitude of the private man." He supported business and the free market, distrusted politicians, railed against the idea of "the masses." He never preached a simpleminded individualism. Indeed, he took it for granted that "the philosopher, the poet, or the religious man will, of course, wish to cast his vote with the democrat, for free trade, for wide suffrage, for the abolition of legal cruelties in the penal code, and for facilitating in every manner the access of the young and the poor to the sources of wealth and power." He despised slavery and taught that divinity grows within each of us. "That which shows God in me, fortifies me," he wrote. "That which shows God out of me, makes me a wart and a wen."

Whenever he describes the power that resides within the autonomous self, his work rings out with eloquent pronouncements—calls to arms, really—about individualism. "Why should we not also enjoy an original relation to the universe?" he asks in his first book, *Nature*. "All that Adam had, all that Caesar could, you have and can do." For the anti-Emerson camp, which includes Hawthorne, Melville (who wrote, "I do not oscillate in Emerson's rainbow"), T. S. Eliot, and Yvor Winters, Emerson's affirmation seems unacceptably positive, but, as Harold Bloom put it, "the mind of Emerson is the mind of America, for worse and for glory, and the central concern of that mind was the American religion, which most memorably was named 'self-reliance.'"

Was Emerson wholeheartedly optimistic about the world? In his journals he wrote, "I like the sayers of No better than the sayers of Yes." And there have always been those who perceived what Henry James called Emerson's "inner reserves and skepticisms, his secret ennuis and ironies." Like Whitman, he contains multitudes. He was a Nietzschean before Nietzsche, a pragmatist before William James, the progenitor of a line of American art that includes Robert Frost and Wallace Stevens, Edward Hopper and Charles Ives, Louis Sullivan and Frank Lloyd Wright. These figures have grasped the undertow in Emerson's thought and the balance beam he walked between imaginative plenitude and spiritual doubt. Emerson staked everything on the idea of self-reliance, but he also called each man "a congress of nations," and the self he exalted is organic and unfixed, something to be invented at the edge of an abyss. That, too, is part of his American ingenuity.

What Emerson said about his Aunt Mary applies to him as well: he, too, is a "Genius always new, subtle, frolicsome, judicial, unpredictable." Wherever we turn in the perpetual American quest for selfhood, Emerson is there ahead of us, urging us to be more creative, beckoning us forward to our own best selves. He is a natural encourager, and I come away from reading him resolved to risk more and do better, to question and affirm. To read him fully is to be thrown into passionate currents and carried away. "I am defeated all the time," he cried out, "yet to victory I am born."

The Imaginary Irish Peasant

A man who does not exist,
A man who is but a dream.

—W. B. Yeats, "The Fisherman"

Throughout the nineteenth century, but particularly in post-famine Ireland, there was an increasing interest in the rural customs and stories of the Irish country people. This interest deeply intensified during the early days of the Irish Literary Revival—indeed, it was in this period that the Irish peasant was fundamentally "created" and characterized for posterity. By placing the peasant figure at the heart of their enterprises, key Revival writers such as W. B. Yeats, John Synge, George Russell (AE), Isabella Augusta Gregory, and Douglas Hyde were participating in a complex cultural discourse motivated by crucial economic, social, and political needs as well as by pressing cultural concerns. They also established the terms of an argument that has affected virtually all subsequent Irish literature. From James Joyce and Flann O'Brien onward, few major Irish writers have not felt compelled to demythologize the peasant figure that was first imagined by the Revivalists. One thinks of Patrick Kavanagh's assertion that his "childhood experience was the usual barbaric life of the Irish country poor," of Sean O'Faolain's vehement contention that the "Noble Peasant is as dead as the Noble Savage," of Seamus Heaney's "archaeological" poems and Michael Longley's three "Mayo Monologues" that implicitly criticize idealizations of Ireland's past and its people, or of the relentlessly bleak vision of Irish rural life and society in John McGahern's first three novels *The Barracks* (1963), *The Dark* (1965), and *The Leavetaking* (1974). One legacy of the Revivalist's glorification of the country people has been a nearly endless intertextual regress in Irish literature.

The romantic myth of the peasant was so powerful that not until the late 1970s and early 1980s did Irish writers systemati-

From *PMLA* (1991): 116–33.

cally begin to interrogate and dismantle the terms of the Revivalist argument, the reductive centering of the country people in Irish literature. Both the Dublin periodical the *Crane Bag* (which started publishing in 1977) and the Field Day Theatre Company (founded in Derry in 1980) have been instrumental in this questioning. In a yearly stage production and in a succession of polemical pamphlets, the directors of Field Day (Brian Friel, Stephen Rea, Seamus Heaney, Tom Paulin, David Hammond, and Seamus Deane), all from Northern Ireland, have set out to "contribute to the solution of the present crisis by producing analyses of the established opinions, myths, and stereotypes which had become both a symptom and a cause of the current situation." One fundamental aspect of this enterprise has been an assault on Irish essentialism, on what Seamus Deane calls "the mystique of Irishness," especially as it has been embodied in an anachronistic Irish culture. In a similar vein the shade of James Joyce advises the pilgrim in Heaney's long poem *Station Island* to "let go, let fly, forget," to relinquish "that subject people stuff," and to fill the element with his own "echo-soundings, searches, probes, allurements." Here Heaney borrows Joyce's voice to advise his own poetic alter ego to break the nets of a debilitating, parasitic Irish cultural discourse.

So who are these Irish country people who have had such a long and controversial history in Irish literature? And precisely what do they represent? I contend that the portraits of the peasant generated by different Irish poets, dramatists, fiction writers, and antiquarians during the Literary Revival were often radically opposed to one another; in fact, each writer undertook to rewrite or to reconceptualize the peasant characters imagined by predecessors and contemporaries. Thus, Yeats and Hyde created portraits of the peasant that not only rivaled each other but aimed primarily at overturning the prevailing English colonial stereotype reflected in the stage Irishman. These portraits were in turn rewritten by Synge, even as Yeats's, Hyde's and Synge's were reworked in divergent ways by Joyce, O'Brien, and Kavanagh. The writers' alternative conceptions, however, were usually underlined by shared assumptions and fictions about rural life. The rural figures delineated by the major Irish authors were so compelling that some readers and critics have mistakenly considered them real or historically accurate. Indeed, each figuration of peasant life claimed a special empirical status for itself, arguing for its own literal verisimilitude. But this supposed empiricism was the brilliant ruse of an elaborate cultural discourse. Beyond their real differences most Irish writers had a common belief in a single undifferentiated entity called "the peasants." This process of turning the peasants into a single figure of literary art ("the peasant") may be termed the "aestheticizing" of the Irish country people. Such aestheticizing takes place whenever a complex historical group of people is necessarily simplified by being collapsed into one entity, "the folk." Yeats's spiritualized fishermen, Synge's wandering tramps, and Joyce's hard and crafty peasants are all emblems of that imaginary entity.

The Irish countryside, however, was populated by a diverse grouping of the rural poor, nearly infinite in its social and economic gradations, that comprised small farmers, laborer-landholders, landless laborers, and itinerant workers. The people themselves made a central distinction not only between large absentee landholders and everyone else but also between those families who owned any land at all and those who did not. The whole concept of an unchanging Irish peasantry has been called into question by F. S. L. Lyons, who suggests that "the general effect of the economic changes (in Ireland) of the second half of the nineteenth century was to substitute a rural bourgeoisie for a rural proletariat." Likewise, Martin J. Waters argues that few aspects of Irish life were unaffected by these massive social and economic transformations: "The notion, then, of an 'Irish peasantry' with a peculiar ethos somehow remaining outside the dynamics of Irish history . . . is untenable." The thirty years between 1860 and 1890 saw a major reordering of the rural class structure. The countryside was permanently altered by the dominant growth of small-farmer proprietorships, the relentless decrease in population in the wake of the famine, and the virtual destruction of a viable Gaelic-speaking community paralleled by a significant growth in English literacy rates. These changes indicate that the countryside was going through something like the last stage of rural proletarianization. Indeed, as Malcolm Brown suggests, the agrarian changes were deep enough to transform the "human nature" of the Irish country people. That peasants no longer existed as such by the time they

were being fiercely "discovered" and portrayed by Irish anti-
quarians and imaginative writers should point up that what
mattered to those writers and their urban audiences was not so
much what peasants were but what they represented. This gap
or disjunction between the imaginary peasant ("a man who
does not exist") and the real country people illuminates the
language that informed both Irish culture and, consequently,
Irish literature.

In the late nineteenth and early twentieth centuries the Irish
peasant was a figure deeply encoded with social, political, and
literary meaning, and to speak or write about that central image
of Irish identity in the context of the time was to participate in a
special kind of cultural discourse. The country people were im-
portant to Irish cultural and political nationalists not for their
own sake but because of what they signified as a concept and as a
language. To speak about the "peasant" was always to speak about
something beyond actual rural life. To debate the characteristics
of that peasant was to share a vocabulary; simultaneously, to un-
dermine and attack someone's idea of the peasant was to come
uncomfortably close to attacking that person's concept of Irish
social classes. So much was at stake in the debate about the people
of the Irish countryside that in essence all the major Irish writers
sought to exchange their own portraits of the peasant for the
larger cultural language and thus to "naturalize" or universalize
their ideas about Irish life. The power of the discourse surround-
ing Irish country life becomes apparent when one remembers
that the most common ethnic stereotype featured in the English
comic weeklies and on the music-hall stage was the Irish peasant,
"Paddy," a comic, quaint, drunken Irish buffoon. But between
1840 and 1890 the portrayal of the stage Irishman changed dra-
matically, and, as L. Perry Curtis Jr. has documented in *Apes and
Angels,* the stereotypes of the late Victorian and early modern era
were far more dangerous than the equivalent caricatures of the
mid-nineteenth century. Largely as a result of heavy postfamine
emigration into the worst English slums, the rise of the Fenian
movement in the 1860s, and the dramatic succession of violent
agrarian revolts in the west of Ireland, the stage Irishman was
reduced in British characterizations to a subhuman figure, a
"white Negro" portrayed in *Punch* as a primitive Frankenstein or
peasant Caliban. Curtis writes:

The gradual but unmistakable transformation of Paddy, the stereo-typical Irish Celt of the mid-nineteenth century, from a drunken and relatively harmless peasant into a dangerous ape-man or sim-ianized agitator reflected a significant shift in the attitudes of some Victorians about the differences between not only Englishmen and Irishmen, but also between human beings and apes.

Nor was the likeness between Irish peasants and subhuman creatures limited to English comic weeklies. The overwhelming squalor and poverty in the West during the horrible years of the famine also led English writers to conclude that the Irish existed on a lower rung of the Darwinian ladder. After traveling through Ireland in 1860, Charles Kingsley, for example, wrote:

> I am haunted by the human chimpanzees I saw along that hun-dred miles of horrible country. I don't believe they are our fault. I believe there are not only more of them than of old, but that they are happier, better, more comfortably fed and lodged under our rule than they ever were. But to see white chimpanzees is dreadful.

To the English public the peasant incarnated the barbarism and savagery of Irish rural life, becoming an emblem of the Irish national character itself. The dehumanization of the Irish in English periodicals (and on the stage) was fiercely challenged by the alternative tradition in Irish newspapers of portraying the peasant as a noble, honest, victimized farmer. No dramatization or portrayal of Irish peasant life could ever be wholly free of the looming shadow and presence of the English colonizer.

The first task of the Irish Literary Revival was to dismantle the Paddy image, invert the stereotype, and make the peasant a spiritual figure, the living embodiment of the "Celtic" imagina-tion, a "natural" aristocrat. The Irish Revivalist writers set out to prove that, in Gregory's polemical words, "Ireland is not the home of buffoonery and of easy sentiment, as it has been repre-sented, but the home of an ancient idealism." That "ancient idealism" was located in the notion of a traditional, unchanging, natural Irish populace. By idealizing peasants—and by defining them as the essence of an ancient, dignified Irish culture—the Revivalists were specifically countering the English stereotype. The supernatural folklore and imaginative wealth of the Irish peasant were also posed against the modern industrial and commercial British spirit. To "sing of old Eire and the ancient ways," as Yeats does in his early poem "To the Rose upon the Rood of Time," was always to sing either explicitly or implicitly against the dominant middle-class English culture. In the tradition of romantic pastoralism, whose terms Raymond Williams has carefully and historically defined in *The Country and the City*, the Revivalists dichotomized urban and rural life, associating cities with "culture" and the countryside with "nature." Similarly, the "naturalness" of folk life was contrasted with the mechanical, material, and industrial development of life in the metropolis. In Ireland the conjunction of pastoralism and romantic nationalism—of projecting an ancient, national, and unchanging Irish peasant culture deep into the past—went arm in arm with the project to "call the Muses home" by creating a contemporary Anglo-Irish literature distinct from Victorian English literature. Thus, Yeats could assert that the dream of the Irish peasant "has never been entangled by reality" and that Anglo-Irish literature, in styling and rooting itself in a tradition of life that existed before commercialism, and the vulgarity founded upon it, was fundamentally opposed to late Victorian and early modern English literature: "Contemporary English literature takes a delight in praising England and her Empire, the masterwork and dream of the middle class." This effort was in turn part of an even larger project to create and define an Irish culture (or an Anglo-Irish culture) distinct from the dominant English culture. In his *Autobiography* Yeats characteristically speaks of half-planning "a new method and a new culture." That project required the writers of the Revival to generate their own precursors—as Jorge Luis Borges says all writers do—to "traditionalize" their work by reviving Irish literary models, consequently locating themselves within an indigenous Irish literary and historical context.

It should not be surprising, then, that as early as 1886 the chief progenitor of the movement, the twenty-one-year-old Yeats, himself newly converted to literary nationalism by John O'Leary, aggressively attacked the "West Britonism" of Edward Dowden (professor of English at Trinity College and "the most distinguished of our critics") and praised Samuel Ferguson as the "greatest Irish poet" for the "barbarous truth" of his writings.

The idea that Irish poetry—of which Ferguson was but one exemplum—was in touch with some kind of deeply savage or primary truth, as opposed to what Yeats called the "leprosy of the modern," was to serve as one of the touchstones of Revival thinking. Ferguson's poetry may in actuality have had less rootedness and savage folk primitivism than Yeats imagined (or wanted to imagine), but it could nonetheless successfully counter the uprooted "luxuriousness" and empty verbal felicities of contemporary rival English poets like Edmund Gosse, Andrew Lang, and Arthur Dobson. Similarly, Yeats discovered the myths and legends of the Irish heroic age in Standish O'Grady's *History of Ireland* (1878–80) and announced that O'Grady's "multifarious knowledge of Gaelic legend and Gaelic history and a most Celtic temperament have put him in communion with the moods that have [always] been over Irish purposes." The contemporary (living) folklore of the Irish countryside and the ancient Gaelic literature (revived by archaeologists and translators) served as dual sources for a new Irish literature. It was Yeats's typcial move to bring them together. Throughout the 1880s and 1890s he created Irish, or Celtic, precursors whom he proclaimed rooted in the ancient folk culture of the Irish peasantry. In this way he was mutating a traditional idea of Irish vitality that was given its key formulation in Matthew Arnold's influential Oxford lectures, *The Study of Celtic Literature* (1867).

Most important for Yeats—as for every major Revival writer to follow—was the necessary linkage of homeland and song. In 1887 he praised Katherine Tynan for writing on Irish subjects, because "in the finding [of] her nationality, she has found also herself." In late-nineteenth-century Ireland "finding yourself" was always tied to finding your national (i.e., non-English) self. If, as Yeats believed, the self could not be wholly circumscribed by nationality, either literary or cultural, neither could it possibly be understood without nationalist referents. What distinguished Irish from English writers was a complex national identity, and in searching for that identity Irish writers turned, as if naturally, to the people they imagined to be most distinctively and authentically Irish: the peasants. This phenomenon helps us to account for the sudden omnipresence of the Irish peasant in late-nineteenth-century Irish literature and for the centrality of folklore to the modern Irish literary imagination.

The idea that the peasant represented some pure state of the national culture was itself a romantic fiction, or an idea that ultimately derived from the philosophy of Herder and the other German Romantics, and it came to most young Irish writers through the compelling personal presence and broad cultural nationalism of John O'Leary. In two important speeches— "What Irishmen Should Know" and "How Irishmen Should Feel"—O'Leary forged the link between indigenous folk forms and the cause of nationalism, specifically arguing that literature and nationality were inseparable and interdependent. O'Leary perceived the nearly inexhaustible possibilities for a new Irish literature based on traditional Irish sources, and, in directing young Irish writers to that untapped reservoir of materials, he was also pointing the way toward a new literature. But the idea that peasants embodied "true" Irish culture had both political and literary currency in the 1840s, when Thomas Davis founded the *Nation* and directed his readers to the folk songs and folkways of their native heritage. (And hence Yeats, who always privileged "literature" over "politics" and the personality of the individual artist over the demands of the audience, found it necessary to carry on a lifelong quarrel—the "de-Davisization" of Irish literature—with a writer whose patriotic poetry he disliked but whom he admired for trying to "speak out of a people to a people.") Yeats, who "began in all things Pre-Raphaelite," was also turned to folklore by William Morris's wedding of social politics and pre-Raphaelite literary forms. Since idealizing the peasantry always had nationalist political as well as cultural implications, the fiction of an original Irish culture incarnated in peasant life motivated not only the development of Anglo-Irish literature but also the emergence of the Gaelic League (1893). Douglas Hyde, its founder and first president, thought of the league as "non-political and non-sectarian," but Padraic Pearse called it, with only partial overstatement, "the most revolutionary influence that has ever come into Ireland." The mythologized peasant also energized the Gaelic Athletic Association (founded by Michael Cusack in 1884), which banned all English games and dances as unpatriotic and "revived" hurley and other Celtic games and pastimes. These democratic movements contributed to the growing revolutionary spirit of what the nationalist editor of the *Leader,* D. P. Moran, dubbed "Irish Ireland." It is not surprising that a newspaper called the *Irish Peasant* emerged between 1903 and 1906, edited for a middle-class Catholic readership by W. P. Ryan, a Gaelic League enthusiast. Peasant life was always projected to the center of the attempt to regenerate and transfigure Ireland.

While most of the important writers and creators of the Irish Literary Revival were Anglo-Irish Protestants (Yeats, Gregory, Synge, Hyde), the rural country people, the "folk" that intensely interested them, were all Catholics. These Anglo-Irish Protestant writers were also separated from a large segment of their own class by their incipient cultural nationalism. For them the Irish peasant not only represented some essential Irish identity but seemed wholly Other, an outlook not shared by urban, middle-class Catholics or by later Catholic writers like Joyce, O'Brien, and Kavanagh. Because the Protestant intellectuals did not see the peasant as a figure out of their own immediate or historical past, they had no trouble in preserving the rural archetype as pagan and primitive rather than as fundamentally Catholic. By mystifying an ancient, unchanging folk life, removed from the harsh realities of land agitation and social conflict in the countryside, they could treat the peasant as a romantic emblem of a deep, cultural, pastoral, and significantly anticommercial (or nonmaterialistic) Irish life. The Revival writers believed that cities, especially English cities like London, represented modernity and commercialism, whereas rural areas, especially the landscape of western Ireland, were free from commerce and materialism. That is, life in the countryside was "natural" and therefore exempt from the material concerns of "culture." Similarly, "individuals" lived in the cities, but the "folk" lived in the country. Thus, the Revival writers projected a group of rural people who were not, to any significant degree, what Yeats called "individuated." Country life was characterized by its orality, organicism, and closeness to nature. By being paganized, the Irish peasant was also turned into a figure of origins, of vital and abundant life freed from the constraints of Christianity and the "moral law." It was a characteristic late-nineteenth-century Irish literary argument (one Yeats used, for example, at his first meeting with the young Joyce) that, to escape from solipsism and abstraction, individual artists should substantiate their work in the communal stories and mythology of the illiterate folk. Deliberate literary artists could escape their own mentality, the highly individualized and potentially sterile "world of ideas," by seeking out the abundant and unself-conscious images of the popular tradition. As Synge put it in his preface to *The Playboy of the Western World:*

> In Ireland, for a few years more, we have a popular imagination that is fiery and magnificent, and tender; so that those of us who wish to write start with a chance that is not given to writers where the springtime of the local life has been forgotten, and the harvest is a memory only, and the straw has been turned to bricks.

It is a corollary to this quest for "rootedness" that the individual artist, almost always a product of town life, could escape the acute self-consciousness of living too much in the mind (what Yeats saw as the fate of the Rhymers) by turning to the popular traditions of people who lived almost exclusively in their bodies and whose folklore seemed to constitute an endless succession of images without ideas. The association of the country with a spiritualized physicality underlined the Revival idea that, in Yeats's words, "all art should be a Centaur finding in the popular lore its back and its strong legs." Also implicit was the belief that the natural popular tradition itself lacked discriminating intelligence and, to achieve greatness, or culture, required that shaping hand of a literary artist. As Yeats formulated this notion to Joyce, "When the idea which comes from individual life marries the image that is born from the people one gets great art, the art of Homer, and of Shakespeare, and of Chartres Cathedral." With this concept in mind one can understand the structure of feelings behind Yeats's celebrated stanza in "The Municipal Gallery Revisited":

> John Synge, I and Augusta Gregory, thought
> All that we did, all that we said or sang
> Must come from contact with the soil, from that
> Contact everything Antaeus-like grew strong.
> We three alone in modern times had brought
> Everything down to that sole test again,
> Dream of the noble and the beggar-man.

The final three lines of this stanza emphasize the heroic isolation and shared ideology of Yeats, Synge, and Gregory ("we . . .

alone in modern times") as well as the essential traditional purity of an enterprise that once more brings "everything down to that sole test." At the same time, a literary ideal is translated into terms that resonate with a (nostalgic) politics of patronage. These lines specifically exclude the large group of nationalist Catholic Dubliners who also thought that everything originally Irish came from contact with the soil but whose political and economic aspirations had little to do with a "dream of the noble and the beggar-man."

Although most of the Irish Literary Revival writers were Anglo-Irish Protestants, most of their home audience—the audience that frequented the Abbey Theatre, for example—was composed of middle-class Catholics. This new Catholic middle class formed a ready market for Irish literature in English and played a key role in the origins and rapid development of the Literary Revival. But Catholics, especially middle-class Catholics, associated the peasant with a strong and debilitating sense of cultural inferiority, and they were at least partially ashamed of their own rural background. The country people never referred to themselves as "peasants" constituting a "peasantry," terms they found derogatory and condescending. In Seamus O'Kelly's novel *Wet Clay* (1922), for example, a young American returns to Ireland to learn the ways of the land. In one scene he tells his cousin, an Irish farmer, and his Gaelic-speaking grandmother that he has followed his blood and become a peasant:

> "A what?" the old woman asked.
> "A peasant—we're all peasants, are we not?"
> "Faith, I never knew that until you came across the ocean to tell us," the old woman said.

The Irish farmer then explains to the American:

> "We never call ourselves peasants. It was always The People. Take the wording of our ritual: 'The Land for the People.' 'The People's Rights.' 'Clear the Ranches of the Cattle; Make Room for the People.' "

The word *peasant* was also in disrepute in middle-class Catholic Dublin, because for middle-class Catholic Dubliners the so-called peasant was almost always a figure out of their own recent family past. Many Catholic Dubliners affected English manners, styles, and habits, stigmatizing the Gaelic language and peasant customs as a badge of social inferiority and backwardness. Their insecurity suggests that as colonials they had internalized English attitudes and stereotypes. But, because they were also nationalists, they liked to idealize and sentimentalize their roots, and they were especially vulnerable when attacked for their "West Britonism." This new Anglicization left the Catholic Dubliners with the painful feeling that they had no identity, that they had lost their native culture without being subsumed by English customs and culture. The sense of belonging to a fragmented or broken culture is famously summed up in Stephen Dedalus's discussion with the English dean of studies in *A Portrait of the Artist as a Young Man:*

> The language in which we are speaking is his before it is mine. How different are the words *home, Christ, ale, master,* on his lips and on mine! I cannot speak or write these words without unrest of spirit. His language, so familiar and so foreign, will always be for me an acquired speech. I have not made or accepted its words. My voice holds them at bay. My soul frets in the shadow of his language.

One way to deal with a debilitating sense of cultural alienation was to turn a Joycean arrogance against Ireland's native culture. Another way was to engage in a permanent conflict with that culture. Dedalus's diary entry on the penultimate page of *Portrait* summons up the old man that Mulrennan had interviewed in the west of Ireland:

> I fear him. I fear his redrimmed horny eyes. It is with him I must struggle all through this night till day come, till he or I lie dead, gripping him by the sinewy throat till . . . Till what? Till he yield to me? No. I mean him no harm.

That old man in a mountain cabin is whom (and what) Dedalus is fleeing.

A more commonly "patriotic" path was the idealization of the native culture. Because urban Catholics were sensitive about belonging to an "inferior" culture, many of them were especially susceptible to pleas, like Douglas Hyde's, to "cultivate what they

have rejected, and build up an Irish nation on Irish lines."
Hyde's influential speech "The Necessity for De-Anglicising Ire-
land" (1892) was powerful because it pinpointed—though not
exclusively for Catholics—the typical ambivalence of people
who had ceased "to be Irish without becoming English":

> It is a fact, and we must face it as a fact, that although they adopt
> English habits and copy England in every way, the great bulk of
> Irishmen and Irishwomen over the whole world are known to be
> filled with a dull, ever-abiding animosity against her, and—right
> or wrong—to grieve when she prospers, and joy when she is hurt.

In her autobiography the Anglo-Irish writer Elizabeth Bowen
makes the useful observation that, whereas the politicians had
promised and failed to deliver Ireland for the Irish, "Irishness
for the Irish was the Gaelic League's promise, subtler and more
essential."

Lower-middle-class and middle-class Catholics in Dublin
shared a discomfort with peasant life as all too Irish, but at the
same time they idealized that life (the rise of the Gaelic
League and the mass appeal of the Gaelic Athletic Association
were in some ways manifestations of that idealization). They
understood that the peasant could be turned into an emblem
not only of Ireland's victimization and nobility but also of its
ignorance, vulgarity, and shame. As George Watson notes,
many middle-class Catholics, who had a basic evolutionary idea
of their own progress, "did not *like* being reminded that Ire-
land was an overwhelmingly rural and peasant society." Again,
the structure of urban feelings associated with peasant life is
made clear in *Portrait* when Dedalus thinks of an emblematic
peasant woman first as a "type of her race and his own" (thus
associating himself with the woman) and then as "a batlike soul
waking in consciousness of itself in darkness and secrecy and
loneliness." In Dedalus's view the woman is a figure of the Irish
unconscious associated with something dark, lonely, beckon-
ing, shameful. The engendering of the peasant is crucial here.
Whereas the colonizer is associated with invulnerable mascu-
line strength, the colonized is associated with a guilty and dan-
gerous female secrecy and vulnerability. "Worst of all," as
Deane says in summarizing the colonial stereotypes of the bar-

baric Irish peasant, "he is sometimes a she." Edna O'Brien summons up a host of conventional associations when she characterizes Ireland as "a woman, a womb, a cave, a cow, a Rosaleen, a sow, a bride, a harlot, and, of course, the Hag of Beare." This engendering was also part of Catholic Dublin's painful ambivalence about peasant life.

For the Catholic middle class, however, the Irish country person functioned as a particularly important autochthonous myth, the source of all authentic Irish life. The peasants symbolized colonial dissent: because they were physically rooted in Irish soil, they established irrefutable property rights and economic claims to Ireland against the English colonizer. Michael Davitt's Land League, founded in 1879, distinctly fostered and powerfully motivated this economic myth. The Land League argued that the peasants had once owned all the land in Celtic Ireland before they were displaced by English settlers. By projecting an economic aspiration for the future into the ancient past, the league helped to politicize the country people around the idea of their historical rights to the land. The league strengthened the concept of the peasant as a victim of English imperialism. Consequently, it spurred and escalated the breakdown of the countryside from a realm of large estates to one of small plots and landholdings, in the process yoking the agrarian reform movement to the nationalist enterprise. The Land League's propaganda was also effective in reversing and inverting the figure of the "primitive" peasant. This economic myth of the peasant differed from the myth of the peasant promulgated by the Anglo-Irish Protestant Revivalists, who spiritualized the peasants by dematerializing them, turning them into an emblem of natural, antieconomic people. So, too, did the paganization of the peasant depart from the middle class's necessary view of an orthodox, unimpeachable peasant Catholicism. In this way the peasant figure was invested with divergent interests and values.

The middle-class Catholics of Dublin formed a ready audience for the Irish theater movement because the idealization of the peasant instilled a sense of pride in a native culture and fit in well with their social and economic aspirations. The move to cultural nationalism was especially significant in the demoralized wake of Charles Parnell's fall from power and the sudden impossibility of parliamentary reform (home rule). As Yeats often testified, the literary movement itself crystallized after the bitter controversy over the Parnell tragedy:

> The modern literature of Ireland, and indeed all that stir of thought which prepared for the Anglo-Irish war began when Parnell fell from power. A disillusioned and embittered Ireland turned from parliamentary politics; an event was conceived and the race began, as I think, to be troubled by that event's long gestation.

In Hugh Hunt's words, "Ireland's national theater was born of a short-lived marriage between political and cultural nationalism in the form of the Celtic . . . Revival." Thus was a constellation of Anglo-Irish Protestant writers and middle-class Catholic nationalists brought together. However, the Catholic audience for that new modern literature could easily feel betrayed by Anglo-Irish Protestant writers who had a significantly different structure of feelings about Irish life. Certainly this attitude helps to account for the enthusiastic creation and welcome development of the National Theatre, which was then riddled with controversies over plays like *The Countless Cathleen, In the Shadow of the Glen,* and *The Playboy of the Western World.* All these controversies centered on the dramatization of the Irish peasant. In their 1906 pamphlet *Irish Plays,* for example, the Abbey playwrights suggested that they had broken with previous stagings of traditional Irish life and had instead "taken their types and scenes direct from Irish life itself":

> This life is rich in dramatic materials, while the Irish peasantry of the hills and coast speak an exuberant language, and have a primitive grace and wildness, due to the wild country they live in, which gives their most ordinary life a vividness and colour unknown in more civilised places.

Consequently, the recurrent objection to these plays and to Synge's work in particular was that, in Daniel Corkery's summary charge, the "plays were not Irish plays inasmuch as they misrepresented the Irish peasant." The special viciousness and bitter frequency with which this charge was leveled at Synge suggest that to "represent" or "misrepresent" the peasant was to project or call into question one's own essential Irish identity. But all representations were in some ways misrepresentations. The very idea that some nonindividuated or typical Irish peasant existed was itself a necessary urban fiction.

The complex literary, social, and political matrix of feelings about Irish rural life provides a historical perspective on the peasant's figuration by five major Irish writers: Yeats, Synge, Joyce, O'Brien, and Kavanagh. Each of these writers created an imaginary peasant in opposition both to the idealized peasant of middle-class Catholic Dublin and to the peasant figures portrayed by previous writers. Similarly, each justified his project by satirizing earlier models of peasant life and positing his own as an empirical reality. This pretense to realism was a way of invoking "presence" and giving special authority to one's own view of Irish country life. In effect, each writer was turning a personal mythology into a national public code and moving an otherwise marginal literary activity into the center of Irish culture. The heavy critical emphasis on Yeats's late Romanticism and Joyce's innovative European modernism has sometimes obscured the need to understand the national public code—the language of Irish culture—if one is to read modern Irish literature.

Yeats's early work was a daring and major refiguration of the Irish peasant. Indeed, every Irish writer since Yeats has had to contend with his revisionary portrait. In a wide variety of songs and ballads, plays and stories, folktale collections, literary sketches, reviews, and essays, Yeats dramatically reversed the stereotype by radically spiritualizing the native country people. His prolific early work publicizes and rethinks the peasant of nineteenth-century antiquarians like Thomas Crofton Croker and fiction writers like William Carleton, revises the (reductively) political peasant of Thomas Davis and the other writers of the Young Ireland Movement, and empiricizes his occult and romantic interests in a rural community. Folklore provided Yeats with the public material for other systems of correspondence as well as for his own private symbol system. As a writer committed to imaginative nationalism, Yeats used the unmined body of Irish materials to root an idiosyncratic symbol system in a common and communal mythology, in effect tying his work to the efforts of writers and scholars all over Ireland. As an Anglo-Irish Protestant, a cultural nationalist, and a romantic occultist in search of a truer faith than Christianity, Yeats discovered in folklore a way to locate his work in a historically "real" community. And so his unique syncretism of romantic and occult ideas conjoined with a culture's interest in national folklore. In Poundian terms, and despite his own highly personal and evolving philosophy, Yeats was working at the center of an Irish vortex.

Synge's ethnographic and dramatic work stands as a second major literary refiguration of the peasant. Indeed, almost all Synge's work is dependent on his rewriting of the Irish country people. Defining the Literary Revival, Synge writes, "The intellectual movement that has taken place in Ireland for the last twenty years has been chiefly a movement towards a nearer appreciation of the country people, and their language." Synge's work begins with a Darwinian shock of recognition, and his journey to the Aran Islands represents a quest for a natural community to replace an absent center, the death of a transcendental god. Synge shared with Yeats an ideology of romantic primitivism, but his stories of the wildness, violence, cruelty, and verbal extravagance at the heart of peasant life subtly revised the way in which the peasant had been previously spiritualized. His ethnography of the Aran Islands and his later efforts to get away from a purely "Cuchulainoid" national theater, especially in his brilliant *Playboy of the Western World,* were also attempts both to revise the Yeatsian spiritualization of the peasant and to undermine and attack the urban middle class's flattened portrait of the noble Irish farmer (an inversion of the stage stereotype). At the same time, Synge's work continued to romanticize the naturalness, paganism, and rich linguistic plenitude of Irish peasant life. For Synge, the peasant served as a substitute or metonym for some original, authentic "human nature." As Yeats's poem "In Memory of Major Robert Gregory" suggests, Synge believed he had come

> Towards nightfall upon certain set apart
> In a most desolate stony place,
> Towards nightfall upon a race
> Passionate and simple like his heart.

Similarly, Synge writes, "I felt that this little corner on the face of the world, and the people who live in it, have a peace and a dignity from which we are shut for ever."

Joyce's strategic literary move—his contribution to the discourse about the peasant—was a glancing demystification of the figure. In a key argument with the nationalist Madden in *Stephen Hero,* Joyce's autobiographical stand-in denies the uniqueness of the Irish peasant: "One would imagine the country was inhabited by cherubim. Damme if I see much difference in peasants: they all seem to me as like one another as a peascod is like another peascod."

When Madden speaks of the "admirable type of culture" and the "simple life" of the peasant, Daedalus counterposes the "mental swamp" of the same peasant: "a life of dull routine—the calculation of coppers, the weekly debauch and weekly piety—a life lived in cunning and fear between the shadows of the parish chapel and the asylum!" The ways in which the peasant's closeness to nature had been romanticized were undoubtedly hovering in the background when Joyce sent Daedalus into a railway car to encounter the "offensive" smell and "odour of debasing humanity." Less convincing is the later affirmative statement that "it was in the constant observance of the peasantry that Stephen chiefly delighted," though the passage does show something of Joyce's ambivalence. For Daedalus—as for Joyce himself—the peasant is distanced as a completely different physical type, someone wholly Other.

The grossness of an all too physical peasant in *Stephen Hero* and *Portrait* was a direct attack on the nationalists, but it was also a sideways revision of the Yeatsian mystifications of peasant life that encompassed Synge as well. For example, Arthur Power reports Joyce's opinion of Synge's work:

> I do not care for it, he told me, for I think that he wrote a kind of fabricated language as unreal as his characters were unreal. Also in my experience the peasants in Ireland are a very different people from what he made them out to be, a hard, crafty and matter-of-fact lot, and I never heard any of them using the language which Synge puts in their mouths.

Similarly, the Cyclops episode of *Ulysses* permanently and mercilessly set out to expose the racism and provincialism of the Citizen's patriotic idea of a Gaelic-speaking peasantry that he knew nothing about. (The model for the Citizen, Michael

Cusack, may be read as an emblem of the Irish Ireland movement itself.) But to rematerialize and re-Catholicize the overly spiritualized peasant of the Celtic twilight, Joyce flattened the peasant's character, describing it as crassly materialistic and slavishly superstitious, totally lacking in redeeming virtues or values. Joyce himself subtly revised this view—and deepened his sense of the "primitive" life in the west of Ireland—in "The Dead." Indeed, the dichotomy between the "overcivilized" city (the East, Dublin) and the passionate, underdeveloped country (the West, Connacht, the Aran Isles) is paramount to any readings of "The Dead." In some fundamental way, Joyce was not primarily interested in rendering life in the countryside; rather, he was fully preoccupied with the embracing humanity and "scrupulous meanness" of a city like Dublin. But it is a sign of the power of the national cultural discourse in Ireland that he nonetheless found it necessary to project and dismantle the central figure of the Irish peasant.

O'Brien's extravagant antipastoral comedies may be read as a fourth stage in the successive literary refigurations of the peasant. Fluent in Gaelic, O'Brien was an accomplished, idiosyncratic stylist of the language who characteristically used his linguistic skills to parody and unmask previous portraits of peasant life. By taking Myles na Gopaleen as his nom de plume—the name of the most despised of nineteenth-century music-hall buffoons, the character from Dion Boucicault's Irish stage melodrama *The Colleen Bawn*—he mockingly reversed the traditional stereotype and turned the satirized into the satirist, the comic figure into the author himself. As Myles, O'Brien witheringly parodied the various sentimentalizations of the peasant in Irish cultural discourse, including a popular spate of autobiographies by country people. Especially galled by Synge's work, he took Joyce's distaste one step further and asserted that "nothing in the whole galaxy of fake is comparable with Synge . . . Playing up to the foreigner, putting up the witty celtic act, doing the erratic but lovable playboy, pretending to be morose and obsessed and thoughtful—all that is wearing so thin that we must put it aside soon in shame as one puts aside a threadbare suit." Myles's strategy was to collapse the British music-hall Paddy and Synge's revisionary portrait.

The enormous gap between the Gaelic League's idealized

peasant and the harsh reality of rural life is the given subject of Myles's novel in Irish, *An Béal Bocht* (*The Poor Mouth*). The author continually returns to the misery of the country people and the squalor of their living conditions, and he mercilessly sends up the sentimentalized poverty portrayed by folklorists and nationalists—"the very best poverty, hunger and distress":

> It had always been said that accuracy of Gaelic (as well as holiness of spirit) grew in proportion to one's lack of worldly goods and since we had the choicest poverty and calamity, we did not understand why the scholars were interested in any half-awkward, perverse Gaelic which was audible in other parts.

O'Brien's other fiction is also obsessed with the falsifications of Irish cultural and political nationalism; indeed, his tour de force, *At-Swim-Two-Birds*, fully enacts the Irish writer's preoccupation with rewriting Irish mythology. If O'Brien lacks an international reputation, the reason may be that his work concentrates on dismantling the literature of Ireland rather than on creating a revisionary "European" oeuvre equal to the poems of Yeats, the plays of Synge, or the fiction of Joyce. While Samuel Beckett is the post-Joycean Irish writer whose work most successfully avoids the constraints of a defining Irish literary tradition by radically denying any antiquarian referents ("not for me all these Deirdres and Maeves and Cathleens," he says repeatedly), O'Brien is the writer whose fiction is most dependent for its effects on previous Irish literary tradition. He has the fate of being the most major belated prose writer to stay in Ireland.

Kavanagh's adversarial relation to the Revival parallels O'Brien's, for both writers felt savage indignation over the literary falsifications of Irish rural life. As the son of a shoemaker in Inniskeene, county Conoghan, as a self-educated Catholic poet who grew up in the countryside, and as a Northern Irish parish writer who was often condescended to as a peasant poet during his years in Dublin (especially after the false pastoralism of his first book, *Ploughman and Other Poems* [1936]), Kavanagh entered the discourse of Irish literature with a deep insecurity and a furious sense of belatedness. "My misfortune as a writer," he once declared, "was that atrocious formula which was invented by Synge and his followers to produce an Irish literature." Kavanagh particularly despised Synge's peasants as "picturesque conventions" speaking a phony language, and he argued that the playwright provided "Irish Protestants who are worried about being 'Irish' with an artificial country." In his autobiography he advanced the argument by asserting that the entire "so-called Irish Literary Movement which purported to be Irish and racy of the Celtic soil was a thorough going English-bred lie." Only by destroying the persistent Revivalist fictions about rural life could Kavanagh clear a space for his own indigenous poems.

In a major antipastoral work, "The Great Hunger" (1942), Kavanagh paints a harsh, revisionary portrait of life in the Irish countryside as economically oppressive, sexually repressed, and emotionally stunted. It simultaneously indicts the brutalities of small-farm life and attacks Revivalist sentimentalizations of that life. Kavanagh's main character, Patrick Maguire, is a rural incarnation of Joyce's spiritually paralyzed characters in *Dubliners*. In the thirteenth section of the poem Kavanagh satirizes the idea of a contented, illiterate peasant who has no worries and who plows and sows in "his little lyrical fields." The second stanza takes aim directly at Yeats's "Municipal Gallery Revisited":

> *There* is the source from which all cultures rise,
> And all religions,
> *There* is the pool in which the poet dips
> And the musician.
> Without the peasant base civilisation must die,
> Unless the clay is in the mouth the singer's singing is useless.

Kavanagh's poem is a full-scale Joycean assault on the idea of the peasant as "the unspoiled child of Prophecy," as the source of all value and virtue, as a natural man "only one remove from the beasts he drives."

Kavanagh further developed his ethnographic poetics in his rural novel *Tarry Flynn* (1948) and in his two books of poems, *A Soul for Sale* (1947) and *Come Dance with Kitty Stobling* (1960). Kavanagh's famous distinction between parochialism and provincialism animates all his mature work: whereas the provincial tries to live "by other people's lines," the parochial relies on self-sufficiency and a fully grounded vision. Heaney has argued that there is a subtle sea change in Kavanagh's later work, especially in his poem "Epic" and in his Canal Bank Sonnets. Heaney's view is that in these poems Kavanagh's places exist less as "documentary geography" than as "transfigured images, sites where the mind projects its own force." It is the meditative intelligence that gives value to the places and not the other way around. Thus Kavanagh, like Heaney himself, becomes more than just a "parishioner of the local."

Kavanagh is the most important Irish poet to follow Yeats, and yet his work has often been overshadowed by Yeats's towering achievement. Because every Irish poet in the past century has been forced to come to terms with the Yeatsian figuration of the Irish peasant, Kavanagh's demystification of the Revivalist myths and his sustained commitment to the unromanticized particulars of rural experience have proved fruitful to subsequent Irish poets. This circumstance also helps to account for the enormous disparity between Kavanagh's reputation outside and inside Ireland. Seldom considered important abroad, Kavanagh's work provided a useful and necessary alternative opening for Irish poets at home, especially for the group of Northern poets who emerged in the 1960s under the tutelage of Philip Hobsbaum: Seamus Heaney, James Simmons, Derek Mahon, Michael Longley, and others. After Kavanagh, it fell to writers with their origins in Ulster, as Fintan O'Toole has written, "to try to show the cruelty and ignorance of the previously idealised peasantry." Thus John Montague's statement that "The Great Hunger" is a poem whose "breathtaking honesty of vision" changed the course of Irish verse rhymes with Deane's idea that Kavanagh "deflected the Yeatsian influence by replacing the notion of the region, Ireland, with the notion of the parish." Deane's idea, in turn, parallels Heaney's statement that "Kavanagh's work probably touches the majority of Irish people more immediately and more intimately than most things in Yeats." What motivates all these affirmations of Kavanagh's importance is the sense that Kavanagh replaced the Literary Revival's romantic pastoralism with a more genuine and ethnographically accurate depiction of rural life.

Yeats, Synge, Joyce, O'Brien, and Kavanagh formulated, destroyed, and reformulated the character of Irish peasant life. Since to reconceptualize the peasant was to control and rewrite the essential Irish image, the source of all authentic Irish culture, each revisionary portrait of the peasant privileged itself and tried to establish its own empirical authenticity by turning culture into nature and thus providing, in Roland Barthes's terms, a natural justification for a historical and literary intention. In other words, each of these five writers projected his own ideological complex of values, beliefs, and feelings into the character of the peasant and then defined (and defended) the figure he had put forward as unchanging and natural. What Barthes states about a tree (a "fact" of nature) may also be applied to the naturalness (the basic "human nature") of the Irish peasant created and re-created by Irish writers:

> Every object in the world can pass from a closed, silent existence to an oral state, open to appropriation by society, for there is no law, whether natural or not, which forbids talking about things. A tree is a tree. Yes, of course. But a tree as expressed by Minou Drouet is no longer quite a tree, it is a tree which is decorated, adapted to a certain type of consumption, laden with literary self-indulgence, revolt, images, in short with a type of social *usage* which is added to pure matter.

The key difference between a tree and a peasant of course is that, in a thousand ways—through their stories, traditions, songs, houses, and customs—the country people can and do speak for themselves. One way to interpret the corpus of their folklore is as a collection of "stories" that they tell to themselves about themselves. The literary sketches, ballads, short stories, plays, political tracts, and romantic ethnographies of the Irish Literary Revival served an equally central but somewhat different function. (The gap between literary renditions of the country people and the country people's stories of themselves can be easily measured by comparing, say, Yeats's *Mythologies* and Synge's *Aran Islands* with memoirs like Tomás O. Crohan's *Islandman* [1929], Maurice O'Sullivan's *Twenty Years A-Growing* [1933], Peig Sayers's *Peig* [1936], and Eric Cross's reminiscence *The Tailor and Ansty* [1942].) The Irish writers' task was not necessarily to create faithful or accurate ethnographic descriptions of rural life, though sometimes their works posed as literary ethnographies. In *The Politics of Landscape,* James Turner puts the matter nicely in terms of rural literature: "Here is the central ideological fact of rural literature: it succeeds as description the more it approaches identity with the world of rural production, but it is meaningful as literature precisely because it is not that world, because it triumphs over and obliterates it." So much was invested in creating the Irish peasant because to speak or write about that figure was always to speak or write about something far beyond the local realities of country life. To turn the peasant into a figure of writing was to participate in an Irish cultural discourse well removed from the world of rural production. It was also to place one's work firmly inside that central national and cultural discourse. By implication, to define an idea of the Irish peasant was to define an idea of Ireland itself.

Federico García Lorca
Poet in the New World

Federico García Lorca's *Poet in New York* (the title was intended as a kind of oxymoron: could a poet manage to live in such a city?) is one of the perplexing classics of twentieth-century poetry. It is a difficult, sometimes bewildered, often hermetic work. It is elusive and enigmatic, mysterious, tortured—a book, to borrow one of the poet's own phrases, "that can baptize in dark water all who look at it." Reading it in the convincing translation by Greg Simon and Steven F. White (1988), one feels the anguished authority and the demonic force and impact of the original. For all its strangeness, Lorca's testament may well be one of the greatest books of poems ever written about New York City—second, perhaps, only to Walt Whitman's powerful embrace of the American megalopolis and comparable in scope and ambition to Hart Crane's magnificent modernist edifice and failed epic *The Bridge*. It might also be called a Spanish *Season in Hell*.

Lorca arrived in New York City in June 1929 and was soon installed in the residence halls at Columbia University, in one or another of which he lived for the next nine months. He was a desultory student of English; indeed, he never learned much of the language, and this increased his sense of being an outsider and viewing the culture through a fractured light. At thirty-one he was already a well-known Spanish literary figure, having published three collections of poems: *Book of Poems* (*Libro de Poemas,* 1921), an apprentice volume of sixty-six lyrics, inspired partly by Juan Ramón Jiménez; a book of radiant *Songs* (*Canciones,* 1927), which combined a native Andalusian music with the tumultu-

---

From the *New Yorker,* 8 August 1988. Reprinted with permission.

ous, metaphorical style characteristic of the avant-garde Hispanic literary movement Ultraísmo; and, finally, the supreme achievement of his early style, the book that caused him so much painful success and "stupid fame" as a so-called gypsy poet—his immensely popular and highly acclaimed *Gypsy Ballads* (*Romancero Gitano*, 1928). Although his New York poems give the impression of a solitary figure wandering the streets alone and living in a dormitory room in complete isolation, his letters to his family reassuringly suggest that he was well tended by a small band of *lorquistas* in the Spanish-speaking intellectual community. This discrepancy between masks confirms that the narrative speaker in *Poet in New York* is as much a poetic invention as Eliot's Tiresias, who has "foresuffered all," or the grandiose self who animates *Leaves of Grass*. He is not so much a fictional character as a concentrated psychological lens through which everything is filtered.

In New York, Lorca experienced an emotional and intellectual crisis. He was tormented by the end of his relationship with the Spanish sculptor Emilio Aladrén and had come abroad partly at least to cut what his letters called the "terrible bonds" of unreciprocated love, with its "sentimental penumbra." His personal unhappiness helps to account for the theme of pure longing and thwarted homosexual love ("dark love") that runs like a vein through *Poet in New York:*

> But I want neither world nor dream, divine voice,
> I want my liberty, my human love
> in the darkest corner of the breeze no one wants.
> My human love!

As Christopher Maurer makes clear in his excellent introduction, the sudden popular success of Lorca's *Gypsy Ballads* intensified his emotional troubles. He protested frequently in letters and interviews that "the gypsies are nothing but a theme" and "this 'gypsy' business gives me an uneducated, uncultured tone and makes me into a 'savage poet,' which . . . I am not." The gossip and rumors about his private life and homosexuality, the gap between what he was ("Sadness over the enigma that I am") and what he seemed in the popular mind to be—all this contributed to a painful loss of equilibrium. This was exacerbated by his estrangement from his friends Salvador Dalí and Luis Buñuel, who were condescending toward the traditionalism of *Gypsy Ballads* and seemed to be conspiring against him. The two filmed *Un Chien Andalou* in Paris in 1929; Lorca heard about the film and told a friend, "Buñuel has made a little shit of a film called 'An Andalusian Dog,' and the 'Andalusian dog' is me."

Lorca's personal history—his prolonged unhappiness and severe depression—unquestionably affected his New York poems. It set the mood and the tone. It also further explains his restless dissatisfaction with his earlier work. By the time he arrived in New York he had made a radical break with his previous style and had embarked upon what he called "my *spiritualized* new manner." In a letter to a friend he confided, "Now I am going to create a poetry that will flow like blood when you cut your wrists, a poetry that has taken leave of reality with an emotion that reflects all my love for things and my joking about things. Love of dying and mockery of dying." That manner has often been mistakenly confused with Surrealism, though Lorca was no more a Surrealist poet than he was a folk poet or a troubadour. He explicitly rejected psychic automatism as a technique and insisted on "the strictest self-awareness" in his creation of images, which had an emotive poetic logic rather than a disembodied rational logic. He wanted "sharp profiles and visible mystery," and his evocative, disconcerting imagery was meant as an intersecting point of contact between his own inner world and the external reality of New York. Although the city is a definite ethnographic presence in *Poet in New York* (one overhears early-morning voices on Riverside Drive, witnesses the crowds at Coney Island and Battery Place at dusk, feels the hovering presence of skyscrapers on Wall Street), everything is transformed by Lorca's phantasmagoric and highly subjective imagery of suffering (as he writes in his "Ode to Walt Whitman:" "Agony, agony, dream, ferment and dream. / This is the world my friend, agony, agony"). The sadness and rage inside him found a correlative in the pessimism and despair of the city during the Great Depression, and New York itself became, in the words he used to describe his own poems, "A passional symbol. Of suffering."

When Lorca read his New York poems aloud, he often invoked the spirit of the *duende*—the word for a Spanish household trickster spirit, but he used it in the Andalusian sense, as a term for the obscure power and demonic inspiration of art. Only with the help of the duende, he felt, could audiences "succeed at the hard task of understanding metaphor" and be able "to hunt, at the speed of the voice, the rhythmic design of the poem." In his groundbreaking essay "Play and Theory of the Duende" he described it as "a mysterious power which everyone senses and no philosopher explains," a scorching "spirit of the earth" that comes only when "death is possible." Each artist fights an irrational, deadly struggle with his own duende. The idea of this force helps to explain not only the "black sounds" and cryptic imagery of *Poet in New York* but also why Lorca considered at one point calling the book *The City* and at another calling it *Introduction to Death*. Death and the city are the twin inspiring presences of the finished work.

Poet in New York is a symphonic cycle of thirty-four poems, a consciously constructed ten-part psychological voyage that begins with an arrival and a descent ("Poems of Solitude at Columbia University") and concludes with a departure ("Flight from New York") followed by an ascent ("The Poet Arrives in Havana"). On one level the book represents—as Lorca once said in a lecture—his "lyrical reaction" to the city, its "extrahuman architecture and furious rhythm," its "geometry and anguish." He had never been abroad before this trip, and he was staggered by what he encountered and witnessed. He was very much an Andalusian in the New World, a sophisticated poet from a provincial place coming to terms with the overwhelming scale and vastness of the city. (He wrote home that "all Granada would fit into three of these buildings.") He was transfixed by what he perceived as "the skyscrapers' battle with the heavens," and the book conveys a sense of being "cut down by the sky" and a longing and nostalgia for the spacious world of childhood. New York is for him a place where during the day people are "mired in numbers and laws, / in mindless games, in fruitless labors" and at dusk are poured into the streets in a human flood. He is personally and culturally disoriented in the crowds and speaks of an unimaginable sadness, of being a "poet without arms, lost / in the vomiting multitude." There is a frenetic quality to the two sections that most consistently evoke the tireless, dehumanized character of the city ("Streets and Dreams" and "Return to the City"). Stylistically, Lorca often relies on large, incantatory free-verse rhythms and repetitions to create a sense of human unreality, of the torments of consciousness, of suffering without end:

> Out in the world, no one sleeps. No one, no one.
> No one sleeps.
> There is a corpse in the farthest graveyard
> complaining for three years
> because of an arid landscape in his knee;
> and a boy who was buried this morning cried so much
> they had to call the dogs to quiet him.

> Life is no dream. Watch out! Watch out! Watch out!
> We fall down stairs and eat the moist earth,
> or we climb to the snow's edge with the choir of dead dahlias.
> But there is no oblivion, no dream:
> raw flesh. Kisses tie mouths
> in a tangle of new veins
> and those who are hurt will hurt without rest
> and those who are frightened by death will carry it on their
>   shoulders.

New York becomes a prototype of the twentieth-century urban world as the poet inveighs against the alienation from nature and the anthropocentrism of city life, the terrible rootlessness of the crowds, the "painful slavery of both men and machines," the racism, the social injustice, and the indifference to suffering that seem to permeate the very atmosphere.

Lorca was deeply empathetic with black life and announced that he "wanted to write the poem of the black race in North America." His ambition is mostly felt in the book's second section, "The Blacks," where the joys of the black aesthetic ("Standards and Paradise of Blacks") and the anguish of black persecution become the central subjects:

> Ay, Harlem! Ay, Harlem! Ay, Harlem!
> There is no anguish like that of your oppressed reds,
> or your blood shuddering with rage inside the dark eclipse,
> or your garnet violence, deaf and dumb in the penumbra,
> or your grand king a prisoner in the uniform of a doorman.

Black life becomes an emblem of the oppression of persecuted outsiders, "the Other." The poet is tortured by the thought of the frenzied suffering around him, "a panorama of open eyes / and bitter inflamed wounds." The blazing city is unquestionably Manhattan, but, as Maurer aptly puts it, the poem "is also the vigil of modern man in quest of the cosmic *meaning* of so much suffering." Thus Lorca mourns the spiritual desolation of the times, a period devoid of any religious consolation. There is only "the world alone in the lonely sky."

The three middle sections of the book compose a kind of solitary rural interlude set in Lake Eden Mills, Vermont, and in the Newburgh, New York, countryside. Lorca called the Vermont landscape "prodigious but infinitely sad," and here, too, the quest for a universal meaning for suffering takes place under the omnipresent sign of death, the nocturnal spaces, the void. The poet is burnished by memories, by an exalted desire for transfiguration ("And I, on the roof's edge, / what a burning angel I look for and am!"; by a dangerous, regressive loss of self:

> I want to cry because I feel like it—
> the way children cry in the last row of seats—
> because I'm not a man, not a poet, not a leaf,
> only a wounded pulse that circles the things of the other side.

The desire for transformation and change is viewed as coterminous with the life force itself, but that, also, is thwarted by the final metamorphosis. Death rules this kingdom with an unchanging and shapeless hand. The only consolation seems to be that the visit to the country has put the poet into renewed contact with the natural world. He returns to the city in a spirit of prophetic denunciation and rages against "the conspiracy / of these deserted offices / that radiate no agony, / that erase the forest plan." His continued spiritual anguish is a kind of psychic hell, and only in the final five poems—two odes and three dance poems—does the speaker begin to climb out of it. In the end he finds a healing refuge in his escape to a rural world (the repeated refrain of the last poem is "I'm going to Santiago"), and he relishes the discovery of a safer, more unified territory in Cuba, the "America with roots." It is hard to resist reading the narrative arc of this journey allegorically, as a story of psychic disintegration and reconstitution, a descent into the abyss and a tentative reemergence.

Poet in New York wasn't published until 1940, four years after the poet's death. A confusing textual history has cast over the book a veil of mystery. It appeared almost simultaneously in a bilingual American edition translated by Rolfe Humphries and in a Mexican edition brought out by Lorca's friend and writer and publisher José Bergamín. Both men were dealing with frustratingly bulky, incomplete manuscripts. These original typescripts are now lost, and for years scholars have argued over the many serious discrepancies between the two editions. Lorca never had a chance to make final revisions or to establish a definitive text. He was unusually resistant to seeing his poems "entombed" on the page (in general his books had to be coaxed out of him) and thought of poetry as an essentially oral art transcribed and translated into the medium of print. Thus the English-speaking reader is twice removed from what Lorca called the "bitter, living poetry" of his New York sequence. His notoriously difficult book has never seemed to me either fiery or cohesive enough in the few previous full translations—useful and admirable but also dated and lacking in colloquial poetic force—such as the Humpries version and Ben Belitt's 1955 edition. This superb translation, also a bilingual edition (with good notes, a helpful textual history, and a translation of Lorca's 1932 lecture on the book, along with the letters that he wrote home to his family), makes it possible for English readers to grapple with an agonistic, inspired work of art.

Together, Greg Simon and Steven F. White have managed to render into a flexible, idiomatic, American-tinged English the various moods of the original. They capture the conversational directness and urgent tempo of Lorca's accusations:

> This isn't a strange place for the dance, I tell you.
> The mask will dance among columns of blood and numbers,
> among hurricanes of gold and groans of the unemployed,
> who will howl, in the dead of night, for your dark time.
> Oh, savage, shameless North America!
> Stretched out on the frontier of snow.

They manage to render faithfully his disembodied conceptual and philosophical unhappiness:

Look at the concrete shapes in search of their void.
Lost dogs and half-eaten apples.
Look at this sad fossil world, with its anxiety and anguish,
a world that can't find the rhythm of its very first sob.

And they find an equivalent rhythm for Lorca's waltzing, sexy,
high-strung, deathward-leaning proclamations of love:

> Little waltz, little waltz, little waltz,
> of itself, of death, and of brandy
> that dips its tail in the sea.
>
> I love you, I love you, I love you,
> with the armchair and the book of death,
> down the melancholy hallway,
> in the iris's darkened garret,
> in our bed that was once the moon's bed,
> and in that dance the turtle dreamed of.
>
> *Ay, ay, ay, ay!*
> Take this broken-waisted waltz.

But, most of all, the translators capture the nervous, hallucinatory intensity of Lorca's imagery and the exclamatory spirit of warning that everywhere animates his sequence ("Wake up. Be still. Listen. Sit up in your bed"). There is a headlong, feverish quality to the verse as the poet tries to find an expressive language equal to his experience of the city—where, for example, millions of animals are slaughtered every day. In the litany of accusations that he calls "New York (Office and Denunciation)" he enumerates the daily slaughter (four million ducks, five million hogs, two thousand pigeons, and so on) and then announces:

> It's better to sob while honing the blade
> or kill dogs on the delirious hunts
> than to resist at dawn
> the endless milk trains,
> the endless blood trains
> and the trains of roses, manacled
> by the dealers in perfume.

The ducks and the pigeons,
and the hogs and the lambs
lay their drops of blood
under the multiplications,
and the terrified bellowing of the cows wrung dry
fills the valley with sorrow
where the Hudson gets drunk on oil.

So intense is the speaker's suffering that at the close of the poem, in a spirit of sacrificial denunciation, he offers himself up as food for the bellowing cows.

Lorca once called his trip to New York "the most useful experience of my life." When he left, he had but six years to live. We are all the more fortunate, then, that he crossed the ocean to the New World. The testament he left behind is a fierce indictment of the modern world incarnated in city life, but it is also a wildly imaginative and joyously alienated declaration of residence—an apocalyptic outcry, a dark, instructive, metaphysical howl of loneliness.

Joseph Cornell
Naked in Arcadia

It often comes as a shock to recall that one of the greatest American artists of this century could, by his own admission, neither draw nor paint. Joseph Cornell didn't make lithographs, sculpt marble, or mold clay. He never attended art school; he had no teachers. He was a collector of bits and scraps, a self-taught virtuoso of childhood, an Emersonian seer who earned a living by selling woolen samples and who spent much of his time scavenging in junk shops and bookstores in quest of the perfect image, the ideal associative chain. He was, by all accounts, excruciatingly shy, a devout Christian Scientist, a solitary who loved penny arcades, Romantic ballerinas, Dutch art, French poetry. As a master of collage, that quintessentially modernist form, he was a representative twentieth-century artist, but there is plenty of evidence to indicate that he saw himself as a nineteenth-century figure marooned in the wrong time. He was a symbolist poet in disguise, a miniaturist who created his lifework in the basement of a modest frame house in Queens that he shared with his mother and an invalid brother. He did not make, as was first said, "toys for adults"; he made time capsules for eternity.

There is something about Cornell's oneiric, homemade work that inspires intimacy, affection, and awe. "We all live in his enchanted forest," John Ashbery wrote in "The Cube Root of Dreams," an appreciation of Cornell's 1967 show at the Guggenheim, and the sentiment resounds. Cornell's descendants include Pop and conceptual artists, entire schools of assemblagists, the last Surrealists, some minimalists—indeed, anyone who cares for mysteries made palpable in a fragile visual space.

From the *New Yorker*, 21 December 1992. Reprinted with permission.

One detects his energizing influence in the stories of Donald Barthelme and Guy Davenport (masters of bric-a-brac and erudition), the experimental movies of Stan Brakhage and Rudy Burckhardt (each collaborated on Cornell's moody, collagist films), the poems of Ashbery and Frank O'Hara (both of whom treat the city as a palimpsest and dwell amid the detritus of language and culture).

Cornell is the most literary of visual artists. His work occupies the shifting, evanescent terrain between word and image, the verbal and the plastic. Both Duchamp and Mondrian considered him a poet; Harold Rosenberg called the shadow boxes "object poems." And poets themselves, the most studious and self-conscious of daydreamers, have always been mesmerized by Cornell's wondrous sea chests. In 1945 Marianne Moore wrote, "His use of early masters and engravers, the sense of design in his wall-paper specimens, and of romance in his choice of woodcuts, his consistent rigor of selection, constitute, it seems to me, a phase of poetry." Dore Ashton has suggested that Cornell's work expresses what was once termed a "poetic soul," and her exemplary collection *A Joseph Cornell Album* (1974) includes four poems dedicated to Cornell: an Ashbery "Pantoum," Stanley Kunitz's "The Crystal Cage" (itself part of a Cornell-like collage), Richard Howard's remarkable confession "Closet Drama" ("The tiny is the last refuge of the tremendous," he writes), and Octavio Paz's "Objects and Apparitions," splendidly translated by Elizabeth Bishop. Paz speaks of Cornell's constructions as "cages for infinity" and as places where "things hurry away from their names," and he concludes:

> Joseph Cornell: inside your boxes
> my words become visible for a moment.

Charles Simic's prose work *Dime-Store Alchemy: The Art of Joseph Cornell* (1992) is the most sustained literary response thus far to Cornell's boxes, montages, and films. It is a poet's book: incisive, freewheeling, dramatic—a mixture of evocation and observation, as lucid and shadowy as the imagination it celebrates. Simic wears his learning lightly. "I have a dream in which Joseph Cornell and I pass each other on the street," he begins, and that sentence—that dream—sets the tone for what follows: a personal quest to approach Cornell through the urban milieu, to encounter and exalt his spirit. Simic writes: "Somewhere in the city of New York there are four or five still unknown objects which belong together. Once together they'll make a work of art. That's Cornell's premise, his metaphysics, and his religion, which I wish to understand."

Dime-Store Alchemy tracks Cornell from a unique angle. Simic—an American poet born in Belgrade and weaned on Surrealism; a writer with an antenna for paradox and a penchant for philosophy; an antic, skeptical visionary ("What a mess!" he has written. "I believe in images as vehicles of transcendence, but I don't believe in God!")—is one of Cornell's most unlikely and most genuine literary heirs. For years, the poet tells us, he tried to approximate Cornell's method, to "make poems from found bits of language." He brings to his task a desire to pursue the collagist's ideas and strategies and a confirmed sense that he is dealing with "an American artist worthy of imitation." The result is a compact book with a large reach, a work that goes on reverberating, like a Duchamp "readymade" or a Mallarmé sonnet.

The book consists of sixty short texts—diverse "illuminations," notebook entries arranged in associative rather than linear fashion, paragraphs put together in tonal blocks that accrue into an homage and a portrait. It is an appreciative assemblage of reveries and meditations, vignettes, memories, lists, and prose poems, quotations from Cornell's copious diaries, and descriptions of the artist's work—his working method—which often read like parables. The pieces range from acute, fairly straightforward mini-essays on Cornell's modernist aims to highly evocative and uncanny responses to the collagist's ideas. Sometimes the two modes are combined, as in "These Are Poets Who Service Church Clocks," which begins with the sociological language "Many people have already speculated about the relationship between play and the sacred" and rises to the ultimate symbolist notion: "Silence is that vast, cosmic church in which we always stand alone. Silence is the only language God speaks."

Simic characteristically proceeds by peering into Cornell's constructions and then describing not only what he sees but where it leads him. "Perhaps the ideal way to observe the boxes is to place them on the floor and lie down beside them," he writes in "Poetics of Miniature," and one pictures him doing precisely that. In this way he becomes a solitary onlooker in a tiny memory theater, gazing at a floodlit stage where time has been permanently suspended. The curtain goes up on a strange play already in progress—Cornell's boxes, like his films, begin in medias res—and the viewer is immediately thrust into a dream world. Simic is so deeply immersed in Cornell's universe that at times he looks right past the actors and into the realm Cornell termed "backstage"—that is, his imagination. In the one-paragraph entry "Cigars Clamped between Their Teeth" Simic writes:

> I've read that Goethe, Hans Christian Andersen, and Lewis Carroll were managers of their own miniature theaters. There must have been many other such playhouses in the world. We study the history and literature of the period, but we know nothing about these plays that were being performed for an audience of one.

He intrudes into Cornell's private sanctum in order to re-create the aura of just such shadow plays.

Simic's response to Cornell is often intuitive and oblique. His meditation may yield an equivalent mood, a kind of light, the look of a place that articulates a parallel reality. Here is "The Magic Study of Happiness":

> In the smallest theater in the world the bread crumbs speak. It's a mystery play on the subject of a lost paradise. Once there was a kitchen with a table on which a few crumbs were left. Through the window you could see your young mother by the fence talking to a neighbor. She was cold and kept hugging her thin dress tighter and tighter. The clouds in the sky sailed on as she threw her head back to laugh.

> Where the words can't go any further—there's the hard table. The crumbs are watching you as you in turn watch them. The unknown in you and the unknown in them attract each other. The two unknowns are like illicit lovers when they're exceedingly and unaccountably happy.

This is Simic's own miniature theater, in which inanimate bread crumbs—the poor leftovers—come to life and speak. It's a fairy-tale kitchen drama that moves offstage to recall a moment of intense domestic happiness, a voyeuristic glimpse of the vulnerable, joyous young mother. This entire scene seems inspired by a constellation of perceptions about the size, scale, and staging of Cornell's work, its deep reverence for the innocence of childhood as well as its Proustian feeling for involuntary memory, for paradise lost and magically recaptured. It illuminates the work's ecstatic, inward nature, how it slips into a range beyond language. What is crucial in Simic's second paragraph is how the solitudes meet and communicate with each other—the secret communion between actor and audience. He dramatizes the way Cornell's boxes activate something immense, lonely, hidden, and almost illicit in the viewer, speaking to him or her with a poignant, blissful intimacy.

As in his poems, Simic's style in *Dime-Store Alchemy* is deceptively offhand and playful, moving fluently between the frontal statement and the indirect suggestion, the ordinary and the metaphysical. In "Dog Wearing Baby Clothes" Simic quotes Cornell's description of more than a hundred and fifty working files:

> a diary journal repository laboratory, picture gallery, museum, sanctuary, observatory, key . . . the core of a labyrinth, a clearinghouse for dreams and visions . . . childhood regained.

Cornell repeatedly sifted these elaborate dossiers in quest of lost time, seeking to recover, in Simic's words, "our old amazement."

The book has eight useful black-and-white illustrations, an abbreviated but deft chronology, and an epigraph from Gérard de Nerval—"Me? I pursue an image, no more"—which, despite its disclaimer, is like a blinking sign that says "Visionary at Work." Simic includes a poem by the Serbian poet Vasko Popa ("Now in the little box / You have the whole world in miniature") and cites passages by Breton, de Chirico, and Magritte, canonical exemplars of mystery. Cornell was himself an artist who referred continually to his own sources. Nerval was his particular hero, the hallucinatory mystic and precursor of the Surrealists, who was famous, as Simic notes, "for promenading the streets of Paris with a live lobster on a leash." The artist also loved Baudelaire, Rimbaud, and Mallarmé, all alchemists of the word. Like Borges, Cornell was conscious of "inventing" his own precursors, who then served as touchstones and sacred figures.

Like Wallace Stevens, he was a stay-at-home who loved the idea of romantic Europe, and especially France—a country he visited often in his mind. "The man who never travelled made up his own Baedeker," Simic writes, and many of the boxes feel like guidebooks in three dimensions, maps to another terrain.

Simic has a humane vision of art as consolation, a certainty that Cornell was trying "to construct a vehicle of reverie, an object that would enrich the imagination of the viewer and keep him company forever." In this book Simic becomes that ideal viewer and recipient, following the artist into imaginary hotels "frequented by phantoms." He watches as Cornell sets out from the family house on Utopia Parkway, knowing that the surveyor of the commonplace is also an interrogator of the ineffable, who isn't sure exactly where he is going or what he is looking for and so desperately needs to find. Perhaps there is a spiritual point where all contradictions can be resolved: "That point is somewhere in the labyrinth and the labyrinth is the city of New York." Simic presents Cornell as a man who basically "walks and looks." He dreams and watches people. In a piece called "The Romantic Movement" Simic summons up the figure of the discharged patient in Poe's story "The Man of the Crowd": "Who among us was not once that pursuer or that stranger?" Simic asks. "Cornell followed shopgirls, waitresses, young students 'who had a look of innocence.' I myself remember a tall man of uncommon handsomeness who walked on Madison Avenue with eyes tightly closed as if he were listening to music." In an entry titled after Wallace Stevens's poem "The Man on the Dump," Simic notes that Cornell "looked the way I imagine Melville's Bartleby to have looked the day he gave up his work to stare at the blank walls outside the office window." For Simic, Cornell resembles no one so much as those familiar-looking strangers in outmoded overcoats who haunt the city like ghosts: "They sit in modest restaurants and side-street cafeterias eating a soft piece of cake. They are deadly pale."

Simic's Cornell is also like Apollinaire ("the poet who loved street performers, musicians with cornets and tambourines, tightrope walkers, jugglers") and Rimbaud ("Arthur, poor boy, you would have walked the length of Fourteenth Street and written many more 'Illuminations' "). For the symbolist poet, eternity has been cut up and scattered into thousands of minuscule pieces. Cornell puts a few of them back together. Simic calls this "the quest for the lost and the beautiful." He writes:

> The disorder of the city is sacred. All things are interrelated. As above, so below. We are fragments of an unutterable whole. Meaning is always in search of itself. Unsuspected revelations await us around the next corner.

Simic believes that, like Whitman, Cornell "saw poetry everywhere." Simic's feeling for this aesthetic imperative and ideal—this way of life, really—is everywhere apparent, since he, too, is a somewhat ironic seeker and witness, an urban lookout. He observes: "On a busy street one quickly becomes a voyeur. An air of danger, eroticism, and crushing solitude plays hide-and-seek in the crowd. The indeterminate, the unforeseeable, the ethereal, and the fleeting rule there."

Once, in a moment of candor, Cornell said, "My work was a natural outcome of my love for the city," and some of Simic's most felicitous passages consider the implications of that basic premise. What he often sees in Cornell's boxes is a freeze-frame of Manhattan in the 1930s, 1940s, or 1950s—Cornell's very productive decades. In a particularly affecting piece the poet peers into a see-through box depicting a window facade and discovers a luminous Hopperesque moment of urban peace:

> Early Sunday morning in June. It had rained after midnight, and the air and the sky have miraculously closed. The avenues are empty and the stores closed. A glimpse of things before anyone has seen them.

Here Simic stands in Cornell's place and describes a city emptied of people, a world refreshed, renewed, and clarified.

Simic's sense of isolation—his memory of being an immigrant—informs not only his reading of Cornell but also his understanding of the country we inhabit. "America is a place where the Old World shipwrecked. Flea markets and garage sales cover the land," he says in "Naked in Arcadia," and goes on:

> They should have made them undress and throw their possessions into the sea for the sake of an America where everybody goes naked, it occurs to me. My parents would be naked, too,

posing for that picture in the Yellowstone Park with my father's much-prized Moroccan red fez.

One of the subtexts of this book is the link between art and loneliness, or, more specifically, the way the wanderer makes what he can out of what he happens upon. The modern artist collects fragments, things that other people throw away. Thus Simic defines an epiphanic instant of poetry: "Three mismatched shoes at the entrance of a dark alley." He recalls the first premise of collage technique—"You don't make art, you find it"—and concludes, "Every art is about the longing of One for the Other. Orphans that we are, we make our sibling kin out of anything we can find."

In "Medici Slot Machine," one of the book's strongest and most charming pieces, and one of the few that take their title from the art, the poet responds to a key work by constructing a separate but analogous universe. The center of Cornell's 1942 construction, his initiating masterwork, is a reproduction of a Renaissance "Portrait of a Young Noble." Black lines crisscross the surface, and the boy stares at us even as we locate him through a telescope lens or a gun sight. He is flanked by fragments of an old map of the Palatine Hill in Rome, which, in turn, are framed by vertical panels of film—strips of Renaissance faces, serial photos of the boy himself. Simic explains:

> The name enchants, and so does the idea—the juxtaposition of the Renaissance boy, the penny arcade, and the Photomat in the subway; what seem at first totally incompatible worlds—but then, of course, we are in Cornell's "magic regions" of Forty-second Street and Times Square.

Simic teases out the implications of the three realms Cornell has radically conjoined, creating a contiguous context for the imagery, daydreaming about the Renaissance princeling in a seedy urban landscape:

> The boy has the face of one lost in reverie who is about to press his forehead against a windowpane. He has no friends. In the subway there are panhandlers, small-time hustlers, drunks, sailors on leave, teen-aged whores loitering about. The air smells of frying oil, popcorn, and urine. The boy-prince studies the Latin

classics and prepares himself for the affairs of the state. He is stubborn and cruel. He already has secret vices. At night he cries himself to sleep.

By projecting outward from the construction, Simic sends the prince—" 'He is as beautiful as a girl,' someone says"—into a hustling, shadowy, eroticized world where "blacks shine shoes, a blind man sells newspapers, young boys in tight jeans hold hands." None of these figures exist in the original box—they are Simic's invention. We follow the androgynous figure into the mirrored world of vending machines and then into the underground cityscape, where he represents "an angelic image in the dark of the subway." Simic's summary statement about the heterogeneous but unified character of the "slot machine" is an ars poetica that applies to the piece we are reading as well as the one we are looking at:

> Whatever it is, it must be ingenious. Our loving gaze can turn it on. A poetry slot machine offering a jackpot of incommensurable meanings activated by our imagination. Its mystic repertoire has many images.

In essence *Dime-Store Alchemy* rotates on the axis of two perceptions of Cornell as a modernist in the American grain: an updated version of Poe and of Dickinson, one metamorphosing into the other. "Cornell and Dickinson are both in the end unknowable," Simic writes. "They live within the riddle, as Dickinson would say. Their biographies explain nothing. They are without precedent, eccentric, original, and thoroughly American."

To appreciate fully Simic's reading of Cornell, you need to look hard again at Cornell's work, to peer into the looking glass of his objects and dream the boxes back into your hands. Reading this book reminded me time and again of the 1980 Cornell retrospective at the Museum of Modern Art. Emerging from that show, one felt the buoyant Americanness of Cornell's work, its totemic innocence and passionate inwardness, its reverence for the wayward magic of city life. It was like being swept back into the world by a giant revelatory wave. "Like a comic-book Spider-Man," Simic writes, "the solitary voyeur rides the web of occult forces."

Dime-Store Alchemy is a meeting of kindred spirits that is itself a work of art and a tribute to a precisionist of longings and enigmas, an explorer who used the quotidiana of the past to investigate the secret recesses of the heart.

Zbigniew Herbert
The Fidelity of Things

"Thus I am in Holland, the kingdom of things, great principality of objects," the Polish poet Zbigniew Herbert jubilantly declares in the first of sixteen "essays and apocryphas" that make up his remarkable book on the golden age of Dutch art, *Still Life with a Bridle* (translated from the Polish by John and Bogdana Carpenter, 1991), and the cry reverberates through the rest of the collection. He is a latter-day pilgrim with a "laconic Baedeker from 1911," a Michelin guide, and a well-thumbed copy of Eugène Fromentin's *Les Maîtres d'Autrefois* (*The Old Masters of Belgium and Holland*), published in 1876, and the object of his pilgrimage is the Netherlands of the imagination, the realm of what he calls his "collective hero": the seventeenth-century Dutch bourgeoisie. For a time he dutifully paces the parquet floors of the great museums and haunts the town squares and clean pavements of once thriving but now out-of-the-way cities, such as Veere, but he feels that the whole experience will be inadequate and somehow sterile if he can't gaze at least once upon the exact, unsullied world of the Dutch Masters.

The problem is that the specific country of three or four centuries ago, so compellingly evoked by thousands of genre paintings, scarcely exists today, or exists only in fragments—in bulging archival files, in the rear stacks of local libraries, and in regional museums of everyday life that display frock coats, kerosene lamps, spinning wheels. The views painted by the Dutch artists of the golden age—the landscapes of the Mannerists Coninxloo and Sebery, the deaf-mute Avercamp, the prodigy Potter, and, of

From the *New Yorker*, 23 December 1991. Reprinted with permission.

course, the towering figures Ruisdael and van Goyen (to name some of Herbert's favorites)—can be seen inside frames on museum walls but hardly anywhere in nature itself. Then, on the way to Rotterdam, in the valley of the River Lek and the River List, Herbert suddenly glimpses the elemental Dutch scene he has been seeking. He sees a valley shaped like a bowl and steeped in damp greens, an ash-colored river, and a group of motionless windmills; thereafter, he carries this view in his memory like a charm. Every now and then, he summons it up, to remind himself that he has journeyed into the interior of Holland and confirmed with his own eyes the reality of the world of the Dutch Masters, a landscape anachronistic and eternal.

"I call on you Old Masters / in hard moments of doubt," Herbert once confessed in a poem, and those hard moments have now ripened into a full-length collection of six independent essays, associatively linked, and ten shorter apocrypha— deliberately marginal commentaries that read as a kind of cross between parables and literary sketches. Herbert's way of attacking a subject is deceptively informal and off-the-cuff—angular and playful—and yet emphatically analytical. His erudition is unpretentious and profound, his style as immaculate as a Delft street or a Vermeer painting. The "semantic transparency" that he has said he seeks in poems is evident in his prose, and, indeed, he shares with the Dutch painters he admires a strong sense of balance and of tact, an imperturbable technical skill, a cleansing visual honesty and forthrightness, an unwavering commitment to a complex clarity. He loves descriptive detail, and the attentive eye is itself one of his primary poetic subjects. "Accuracy is essential," his alter ego Mr. Cogito announces in one poem: a moral imperative.

Zbigniew Herbert is one of the finest and most original writers living in Europe today and one of the greatest Polish writers of this century. He is a figure comparable to, say, T. S. Eliot or W. H. Auden: a classical-minded avant-garde poet, playwright, and essayist who has created a cosmopolitan body of work remarkable for its intellectual and moral astringency. His writing is, to use one well-known designation of it, "eminently sane" in a century and a part of the world that haven't always seemed so. Herbert belongs to a war-torn generation of Polish writers (he was born in Lvov in 1924) sometimes referred to as Kolumbowie, or Columbuses, because, having come of age during the Nazi occupation of Poland and the bitter years of the Stalinist repression, they were subsequently committed to exploring the new postwar reality. But he has written: "Something makes me different from the 'War Generation.' It seems to me that I came away from the war without accepting the failure of the earlier morality. It is still attractive to me most of all because I painfully feel the lack of tablets of values in the contemporary world."

Herbert is a stubbornly idiosyncratic poet of isolation, disinheritance, and grief—what one critic terms "multi-level orphanhood." He is also a poet of "historical irony" (the phrase is Czeslaw Milosz's), continually confronting his own experience and juxtaposing it with the experience of the past, seeking the grounds for what he has called "universal compassion." This most ironic, civilized, and historically conscious of European poets (the exemplary personages in his poems tend to be figures such as Marcus Aurelius and Hamlet, Roman proconsuls and Greek gods) has spent his adulthood in opposition to totalitarian society, and of this he has written in "The Power of Taste":

> It didn't require great character at all our refusal disagreement
>   and resistance
> we had a shred of necessary courage but fundamentally it was a
>   matter of taste
>
> Yes taste in which there are fibers of soul the cartilage of
>   conscience

Herbert has deliberately cultivated a cool, economical, and antirhetorical style, dispensing with punctuation in his poems and suspicious of grand effects—what one poem calls "the piano at the top of the Alps" and "the artificial fires of poetry." He seeks the pristine word that will stand against contemporary debasements of language and describe the world as it is, and this ideal unquestionably informs his enthusiasm for the best of provincial Dutch culture.

Still Life with a Bridle is Herbert's fifth book to be translated into English. Thus far, he has been majestically served by his translators, all of whom note how much texture and resonance is lost in the transposition from Polish into English. True as this is, Herbert does seem to be one of those rare writers, simultaneously modern and classical—like the Greek Alexandrian Constantine Cavafy—with a sardonic wit and a startling intellectual clarity that come through linguistic barriers exceptionally well. To date, there have been two different versions of Herbert's *Selected Poems*—one translated by Milosz and Peter Dale Scott (1968) and one by the wholly admirable Carpenters (1977), who have also given us *Report from the Besieged City* (1985), perhaps the most influential single volume of Polish poetry to appear in the 1980s. Herbert perfected his prose style in *Barbarian in the Garden* (translated by Michael March and Jaroslav Anders [1985]), a book of ten essays that begins in Lascaux and concludes with memories of Valois, taking up along the way such subjects as the ruined Greek temples at Paestum and the construction of French Gothic cathedrals, Orvieto's Duomo and the paintings of Piero della Francesca. *Barbarian in the Garden* is ostensibly a travel book (the author is the so-called barbarian—the outsider, the Eastern European, the Pole—and the sunstruck "garden" is Mediterranean culture), yet it stands in relation to most contemporary travel books the way Frans Hals's group portraits stand in relation to most commissioned portraits of the seventeenth century. Similarly, *Still Life with a Bridle* has as much relation to most art history texts as the Rembrandt painting known as *The Night Watch* has to most seventeenth-century history paintings; that is, Rembrandt's work is not a history painting at all but an imaginative group portrait disguised as one. Composed over a period of many years, the sixteen chapters of *Still Life with a Bridle* are neither a survey nor a definitive study of Dutch painting so much as the well-sifted results of a lifetime of thinking about Dutch art and the culture that fostered and embraced it.

Herbert characteristically approaches seventeenth-century Dutch culture with curiosity, affection, and a good deal of hard-headed pragmatism. One might subtitle each of his pieces "Skeptic at Work," as he seeks the elusive pattern in the tapestry, the articulated skull beneath the smooth skin, the underlying moral. Like a flower painting by Boschaert or a still life by Claesz, Herbert's work presents a surface so cleanly rendered and apparently natural that one might almost miss the careful artifice and arrangement and the emblematic meaning of the whole. Thus, it may take a while to notice that each of Herbert's pieces has the shape of a meditative inquiry. A question is asked and, if possible, answered; a moral proposed, subtly rooted out, and brought home to us. In this way Dutch culture comes to speak across the centuries—an example, a contrast, a reproach.

The questions Herbert asks about Dutch art and life are deceptively simple and in themselves slyly illuminating—the benchmark of his style. For instance, in the first essay he wonders why it is that in Holland objects from daily life have been preserved with an "almost religious attention," and in the last essay he reflects upon the nonheroic and pacifist spirit of Dutch painting. In "The Price of Art" he examines the life of the Dutch Masters from the mundane but revealing vantage point of the financial balance sheet. "It is better and more honest," he tells us of that approach, "than the pathos and sentimental sighs favored by authors of *vies romanceés* written for tender hearts." In one of his best, and funniest, essays he follows "the curve of the tulip fever," seeking the hidden causes of the speculative *tulpenwoede* (tulipomania) that swept the usually sober, parsimonious nation in the 1620s and 1630s. He calls tulipomania "an episode inscribed on the margin of Great History, and admits to a strange preference for "presenting follies in the sanctuaries of reason." With a rhetorical question, however, Herbert then turns an isolated botanical craze into a representative historical episode, a chilling allegory: "For doesn't the affair we have described remind us of other, more dangerous follies of humanity that consist in the irrational attachment to a single idea, a single symbol, or a single formula for happiness?"

Herbert's essay on Gerard Terborch, subtitled "The Discreet Charm of the Bourgeoisie," tries to get at the nature of a painter who seems strikingly idiosyncratic and without precursors and at the same time a product of the Dutch burgher world. It also serves as a companion piece to the title essay, which investigates the mysterious life and work of the painter known as Torrentius, whom he calls "the Orpheus of the still life." An enigmatic figure, possibly a Rosicrucian, with a Socratic bent and a scandalous reputation as a libertine, Torrentius was, Herbert points out, the unhappy precursor of the Marquis de Sade, the nineteenth-century *poétes maudits,* and the Surrealists. Herbert particularly admires the discreet ambiguity, ironic playfulness, and veiled eroticism that he finds in both Terborch and Torrentius: the way their respective masterpieces, *Fatherly Admonition* and

Still Life with a Bridle, appear utterly decorous on the surface even as they suggest secret and illicit symbolic meanings.

Herbert is not the first to point out that Terborch's well-known painting, ostensibly presenting a domestic scene in which a father admonishes his daughter, who has her back turned, while his wife averts her gaze, has in it emblematic elements suggesting that in actuality a soldier may be offering a coin to a haughty young woman while an older woman, perhaps a procuress, stares down into a glass of wine. The paradox of *Fatherly Admonition,* Herbert notes, "consists in showing a morally reprehensible event with irreproachable decorations, saturated with virtue and nobility." He finds a parallel intellectual subtlety at work in the only painting by Torrentius to have survived. *Still Life with a Bridle,* painted on a nearly round panel and dated 1614, is a representational work that creates an oversized, surrealistic effect by placing a group of objects at eye level against an impenetrable black background. A sharp, almost clinical light from an undesignated source illuminates a long-spouted pewter pitcher, a chain bridle, and a large earthenware jug. In front of the bridle a half-filled glass goblet and two porcelain pipes with their bowls turned down are resting on a sheet of music. The inscription on the music page indicates that the work is a hymn to restraint, but as Herbert unpacks the symbolism, interpreting the represented objects and rethinking the inscription, it becomes evident, he suggests, that the painting "should be understood as an apparent allegory of moderation, while in reality, in an intricately camouflaged way, it is the praise of a man liberated from bonds, uncommon, standing high above the crowd of petty philistines." In reading Herbert's analysis of these paintings, one thinks of how he has ironically circumvented the censors in his own poems, mastering the art of ambiguity, suggesting radically different meanings simultaneously.

In *The Embarrassment of Riches,* Simon Schama convincingly argues that the specifically Dutch problem in the seventeenth century was "how to create a moral order *within* a terrestrial paradise." What is it about the Dutch situation in the golden age that seems so usefully resonant and precisely moving to Herbert—a poet who, after all, in the voice of Mr. Cogito speaks of returning to the "stony bosom / of his homeland" and of being "alone / in the treasure-house / of all misfortunes"? Certainly

Herbert is not alone in his admiration of a tiny bourgeois republic that was long ago so politically, economically, and culturally progressive. "In the Europe of the seventeenth century, torn by religious wars, it was an unusual, universally admired asylum of freedom, tolerance, and prosperity," he says. In the wealth of details and observations that Herbert presents about the newly Protestant, newly independent capitalist state, with its growing national consciousness and its strong set of humanistic values, three things seem exemplary and worth stressing: the Dutch love for objects, for paintings, and for freedom. How he weaves these three apparently disparate aspects of Dutch reality together tells us in what way and to what extent the golden age represents for him a moral code and an image of civilization.

The Dutch middle class had a consuming, sometimes inordinate interest in the things of this world. "We know the Dutch loved objects, the worldly reward for industriousness and saving," Herbert reports. They were intensely proud of the material domain that they inhabited and obsessively cleaned and cared for. To put the matter in a somewhat larger frame, they had what the Dutch historian J. H. Huizinga called an "unshakable faith in the reality and importance of all earthly things." Their pride was bound up with their possessions because they were, in Huizinga's words, "firmly convinced of the substantiality of things." The external world they lived in, however, was perilously surrounded by water and subject to disastrous floods—far more liquid and mutable, less stable and solid, then it appeared. Herbert quotes the French Romantic novelist Benjamin Constant: "This brave nation lives with all that it possesses on a volcano, the lava of which is water." It is as if in their devotion to the substantive and material the Dutch were trying to nail down the world, to fix it in place. One function of realistic visual art was to multiply reality, to catch things before they floated away or evaporated. Herbert writes, "The attachment of things was so great that pictures and portraits of objects were commissioned as if to confirm their existence and prolong their lives."

The Dutch liked paintings of all sorts, but they had a special appetite for native landscapes and townscapes, individual and group portraits, floral paintings and still lifes—scenes of everyday life. History paintings and religious scenes certainly existed and were valued highly, but they were minority modes. The burgher audience adored genre paintings—representations of its own world. Fromentin, Herbert's nineteenth-century guide, astutely remarks that the Dutch seemed to take the right to their own school of painting as one of the stipulations of the 1609 treaty with the Spanish. Seventeenth-century travelers to the Netherlands repeatedly commented on the wide popularity of Dutch painting in Dutch life. Herbert notes that it was not uncommon to find one or two hundred paintings in an average affluent, or even less affluent, bourgeois household. There were paintings hanging in town halls and other civic buildings, in offices, orphanages, taverns. One astonished traveler reported seeing an immense number of paintings at the annual Rotterdam fair. Herbert muses that "the very fact of exhibiting them among stalls, clucking chickens, mooing cattle, junk, vegetables, fish, farm products, and household objects must have seemed very peculiar, and was difficult for an average visitor to understand." In point of fact, paintings could be found hanging almost anywhere except in churches. The chief patronage of homegrown Dutch art came neither from the Reformed Church nor from the Court at the Hague but from merchants and shopkeepers, civil officials, small traders, and artisans.

In general, painting in the Netherlands was treated as a craft, its value unquestioned, its place in society universally recognized. "The question why art exists did not occur to anyone," Herbert writes, "because a world without paintings was simply inconceivable." Paintings were cheap and prevalent. Artists belonged to the Guild of Saint Luke, the patron saint of painters, and were subject to and protected by local regulations. Guild membership in no way guaranteed their success or spared them financial difficulties, and, indeed, a depressingly large number, though by no means all, suffered severe economic hardships. Painters often used their own work as currency, and almost anything could be paid for with paintings. Herbert notes, "Loans were secured by pledging paintings; debts (card debts as well) were paid with them, cobblers', butchers', bakers', and tailors' bills were settled with paintings." And, further, with paintings "it was possible to pay off a house, buy a horse and give a dowry to a daughter if the master did not possess any other wealth."

Despite the expansive middle-class market (and the Dutch

were the first to give us an art market where paintings were not only aesthetic objects but a source of capital and speculation), the supply outstripped the demand, and consequently painters tended to specialize in particular subjects. For example, Hobbema concentrated on forest scenes and Willem van de Velde on maritime ones; de Hooch focused on bourgeois interiors and courtyards; the architectural painter Saenredam rendered church interiors and topographical views. Painters also took on all kinds of extra employment, which they did not consider beneath them, to make ends meet. Herbert is especially moved by the craftsmanship and the humility of the Dutch painters, and in contrasting the time with ours he reaches a fever pitch of eloquence: "The old masters—all of them without exception—could repeat after Racine, 'We work to please the public.' Which means they believed in the purposefulness of their work and the possibility of interhuman communication. They affirmed visible reality with an inspired scrupulousness and childish seriousness, as if the order of the world and the revolution of the stars, the permanence of the firmament, depended on it." Herbert's praise of the lovely naïveté of the Dutch Masters is reminiscent of something he once told an interviewer— that the primary enemy of culture is not censorship but nihilism.

The Dutch painters created a kind of realism, but it is not quite accurate to say, as Fromentin does, that for fifty years they simply painted the portrait of Dutch society. The Old Masters had what might be called representational values, but they were not, strictly speaking, naturalists; that is, they organized what they made for visual, emblematic, or symbolic ends. One notorious example is Ruisdael's *The Jewish Cemetery,* so much admired by Goethe, in which the artist romantically painted into the background nonexistent ruins and a dark, wooded landscape. A bouquet of flowers by Bosschaert often includes types that bloom at different times of the year—symbolic of the fleeting nature of life—and an exquisitely rendered church by de Witte turns out to be a composite of several buildings. Yet the Dutch painters obviously placed a very high value on "realistic" surfaces. Their reticence and their impartiality were profound, and they were deeply engaged in the problem of what Svetlana Alpers, in her book on Dutch art, appropriately labels "the art of describing" and the "display of representational craft." Part of what speaks so forcefully and resolutely to Herbert is the Dutch artists' struggle to represent daily life, landscapes with man-made objects in them, ordinary things arrested in time and space.

In his own poems Herbert has repeatedly shown what he calls a "rapacious love of the concrete," a determination to see things as they are, to give them their proper names. "At last the fidelity of things opens our eyes," he declares in his poem "Stool." To the poet who has suffered under, and seen the collapse of, several shameful ideologies, the commitment to concrete particulars stands as a fundamental contrast and direct alternative to the cant and half-truths of human beings. Thus he asserts in the poem "Pebble," "The pebble / is a perfect creature / equal to itself / mindful of its limits," and "its ardour and coldness /are just and full of dignity." He confesses:

> I feel a heavy remorse
> when I hold it in my hand
> and its noble body
> is permeated by false warmth
>
> —Pebbles cannot be tamed
> to the end they will look at us
> with a calm and very clear eye

His radically understated style is a specific corollary to the quest for things-in-themselves.

Yet Herbert's strong aesthetic preference for transparency has sometimes misled readers and critics alike. For all his professed love of the concrete, he isn't a phenomenological poet per se; on the contrary, he is supremely a poet of thought, self-questioning, philosophically self-conscious—a tragic post-Cartesian attracted to Erasmus. As the Carpenters point out in their introduction to *Report from the Besieged City,* many of Herbert's poems address the issues and problems of accurate description—or, as he puts it at the end of one poem, "Don't be surprised we don't know how to describe the world / and only speak to things affectionately by their first names." Herbert's lyrics often return to the textural and ethical problems involved in inscribing and psychologizing experience, in trying to write down the fluctuating external world and be faithful not only to what we know but also to what we don't know. Thus an "uncertain clarity" becomes his primary representational value.

In the title essay Herbert acknowledges that there is something tactless and naive in trying to write about painting, in trying to describe a visual mode by verbal means—an activity, Witold Gombrowicz once wryly told him, that should be left to "scientific" historians of art. Herbert admits, "I know well, too well, all the agonies and vain effort of what is called description, and also the audacity of translating the wonderful language of painting into the language—as voluminous, as receptive as hell—in which court verdicts and love novels are written." Why, then, has he not been able to restrain himself? Because through the medium of painting he found a world where "concepts sprouted only from things," and he could at last speak "the simple language of the elements." Most characteristically, he declares, "How good that the deadly abstractions had not drunk all the blood of reality to the end."

Herbert readily admits to an inability to describe paintings adequately or to convince anyone that a particular work is a masterpiece—especially one such as *Still Life with a Bridle,* which he says, "art historians have not confirmed . . . with their word of honor." He goes on, "I myself do not know how to translate my stifled shout when I first stood face-to-face with the 'Still Life' into comprehensible language, nor the joyous surprise, the gratitude that I was endowed beyond measure, the soaring act of rapture." Yet there are few writers who have given us such strikingly perceptive accounts of the naked encounter with a work of art, one's first, visceral response to a painting as to a person, the way a viewer can feel addressed and beckoned across a room, mesmerized, gripped. Herbert describes this inner state as "a suddenly awakened intense curiosity, sharp concentration with the senses alarmed, hope for an adventure and consent to be dazzled." At times it seems that Herbert longs to become one of the seventeenth-century painters he admires and use a purer medium than language; at the very least he seeks the clarifying directness that he finds in the Old Masters. He could be speaking about any one of a hundred Dutch painters when he writes that Mr. Cogito "valued concrete objects / standing quietly in space," and "he chose / what depends / on earthly measures and judgment."

It is not uncommon for historians to stress the simplicity, the pragmatism, and, some would say, the unimaginative worldliness of seventeenth-century Dutch society, but, as far as I know, Herbert is the only writer to have authoritatively linked the Dutch attachment to material objects, and the specific nature of Dutch painting as well, to a basic, matter-of-fact devotion to freedom. Yet freedom was perhaps the first, unstated tenet of Dutch society, and travelers from other parts of Europe commented repeatedly on how much personal and collective freedom they found in the emerging country. During the eighty years in which the Dutch fought their war of liberation from the Spanish, they also invented a national culture, and through it all they were surprisingly peace loving and nonmilitaristic. Their dislike of force was well-known. Herbert writes: "For the Dutch, war was not a beautiful craft, an adventure of youth or the crowning of a man's life. They undertook it without exaltation but also without protest, as one enters a struggle with an element . . . What was most important was to save: to protect, to spare, and carry from the storm a sane head and one's belongings."

The Dutch are so exemplary to Herbert that when he documents cases of intolerance and persecution, like the shameful charge of impiety brought against Torrentius, they seem all the worse because they take place in "enlightened Holland." *Tulpenwoede* seems all the more poignant because it happens against the backdrop of a tolerant, freedom-loving society. Freedom in Dutch culture was socially ingrained, primarily by custom and secondarily by law. In the seventeenth century, as in our own, freedom was in most places no more than a theoretical concept, a vague abstraction, a subject for political treatises. "But for the Dutch, it was something as simple as breathing, looking, and touching objects," Herbert writes. "It did not need to be defined or beautified. This is why there is no division in their art between what is great and what is small, what is important and unimportant, elevated and ordinary." In effect, Herbert is giving us a defense of democratic art in a golden age: an argument for an aesthetic and moral order.

Who has not stood in the great museums and marveled at the mysterious dailiness of Dutch art, at the scrupulous care and dazzling virtuosity of its makers? Who has not been stopped by its meticulous surfaces and glittering objects, that absorbing northern light? Reading Herbert's essays and apocrypha, one remembers landscapes with enormous skies, seascapes, and waterlogged canals. One thinks of market and tavern scenes, conversation pieces, kitchen paintings. The calm and stillness of Sundays, women combing their children's hair, families making music. Suitors in black coats, young women in white dresses poring over letters. Regents and lacemakers, a man and a woman seated at a virginal, a goldfinch chained to a perch. A spiral staircase by Dou, a tile floor by de Hooch, a patterned table covering by Vermeer. The sheen of apples in a colorful bowl, flowers in a terra-cotta vase. Ordinary objects radiating in space, discrete and luminous, as if speaking for themselves. The light falling across textured maps and open windows, interior courtyards and receding hallways, doors that play ingeniously with interiors and exteriors, with illusions of space, with what is forever inside and outside the house. A clock stopped in mid-beat, a voice in mid-sentence. Still-life with books. Still-life with a bridle.

Aleksander Wat

Songs of a Wanderer

Almost thirteen years ago, while I was rummaging through the back stacks of a bookstore in Ann Arbor, Michigan, I came across a thin, small-press volume of *Mediterranean Poems,* by Aleksander Wat (translated by Czeslaw Milosz, 1977). The book was as blue as the Mediterranean itself, but the name Wat was scalded in white letters across the front. Who was he? One of the cofounders of Polish Futurism, I discovered, a kind of Central European Dadaist of the late 1910s and early 1920s—part Vladimir Mayakovsky, part Tristan Tzara—who had subsequently embraced Communism and then fallen, perhaps inevitably, into the unspeakable abyss of the Stalinist prisons. A former editor of the influential Communist magazine the *Literary Monthly,* and one of the best-known literary figures in Poland, Wat had stopped writing for years but had almost miraculously reemerged as a poet in the mid-1950s, a survivor who had been to the heart of Russia and returned to tell the tale—or a small part of the tale. He had been purged and "rehabilitated"; he had suffered a devastating stroke and traumatic aftereffects; he had gone to live abroad in France and Italy; he had died in 1967.

These were externals. I had read a few fragmentary poems by Wat in Czeslaw Milosz's anthology *Postwar Polish Poetry,* but their significance had escaped me. (So, too, I knew the work of a trio of great postwar Polish poets—Tadeusz Rozewicz, Zbigniew Herbert, and, of course, Milosz himself—and I would today add Wislawa Szymborska to the list.) Yet I was unprepared for the playful sorrows and disturbing inconsistencies of Wat's voice, for his philosophical depths and metaphysical aspirations, his specu-

From the *New Yorker,* 16 July 1990. Reprinted with permission.

lative seriousness, his sad buffooneries and torments. Nor was I prepared for the sheer accumulated weight of suffering in the poems. He spoke with perfect candor from limitless depths of unhappiness. His work seemed propelled by a desire—by a full-scale need, really—to escape from the excruciating burden of consciousness, to flee from the human. One poem began:

> To be a mouse. Preferably a field mouse. Or a garden mouse—
> but not the kind that live in houses.
> Man exudes an abominable smell!
> We all know it—birds, crabs, rats.
> He provokes disgust and fear.
>
> Trembling.

Another announced flatly, "There is no salvation"; a third, "A Damned Man," concluded, "I always knew I would come to a bad end." The second section of "Songs of a Wanderer" spoke matter-of-factly about being "disgusted by everything alive"; the fourth section ended with the image of "manure, mycosis, rot, the agony of things living and not living." The agony was wrenching, headlong, irremediable. In "Dreams from the Shore of the Mediterranean," he was a Hamlet haunted by his own bad dreams, a patient in a Warsaw clinic nicknamed Siberia, a fallen prophet who had stumbled into a modern Sidon, lashing out against the populace:

> All of you are deaf and dumb in this city.
> In the damned city. In this city
> you are damned. In a sentenced city. Forever.

These poems read like the jottings of a European Job crying out from inside the broken walls of his body. He is crippled by pain. He has journeyed to the demonic heart of our century and come back to declare in a calm voice, "There is no bottom to evil."

Mediterranean Poems has now been substantially revised and enlarged and incorporated into a fuller and more definitive volume, *With the Skin: Poems of Aleksander Wat* (translated by Czeslaw Milosz and Leonard Nathan, 1990). This edition contains the bulk of three of Wat's books: *Poems* (1957), *Mediterranean*

Poems (1962), and *Dark Trinket* (1968), a posthumously published collection of poems from 1963 to 1967. Wat is virtually unknown as a poet in the West and is mostly forgotten as an intellectual figure. This obscurity has persisted despite the fact that Milosz—arguably the greatest poet of our era—not only has translated and collaborated in retranslating Wat's poems but also has written about Wat in all three editions of *Postwar Polish Poetry;* in *The Witness of Poetry,* his Charles Eliot Norton Lectures, at Harvard, for 1981–82; in his monumental *History of Polish Literature;* in the piece entitled "On Modern Russian Literature and the West," in his book of essays *Emperor of the Earth: Modes of Eccentric Vision;* in his foreword to Lillian Vallee's new translation of Wat's sole book of short stories, *Lucifer Unemployed;* in his translator's foreword to *Mediterranean Poems;* in a formal introduction to *With the Skin* and in a lively, informal conversation between the cotranslators that serves as an afterword to it; and in his substantive foreword to Wat's spellbinding memoir *My Century: The Odyssey of a Polish Intellectual* (edited and translated by Richard Lourie, 1988), a series of conversations that Milosz conducted and tape-recorded with Wat in Berkeley in the mid-1960s. These conversations worked so well not only because Milosz knew precisely what to ask but because Wat, eleven years his senior, desperately needed to tell his story to someone who both wanted to hear it and shared his frame of reference. The two Polish poets—one formed by the 1920s, the other by the 1930s—also shared a compulsion to remember, to summon up the body of a lost world, a forgotten kingdom. Here is "What Once Was Great," Milosz's compelling lyric about the diminishments of history—his variation on "Ozymandias"—dedicated to Wat and his wife:

> What once was great, now appeared small.
> Kingdoms were fading like snow-covered bronze.
>
> What once could smite, now smites no more.
> Celestial earths roll on and shine.
>
> Stretched on the grass by the bank of a river,
> As long, long ago, I launch my boats of bark.

Czeslaw Milosz has done a good deal; indeed, he has been fairly obsessed with keeping alive the memory of a friend who, as he says, "experienced the philosophies of the twentieth century bodily, in their most tangible forms." Wat's work exists in that intense zone where poetry, history, and metaphysics intersect.

Aleksander Wat belonged to a generation that grew up with the century and was shaped by its various traumas and cataclysms. History, as he said in so many different ways, was inscribed into his skin. He was born in Warsaw on May Day, 1890, into an assimilated intellectual Jewish family—the family name was Chwat—with a fatal dual allegiance to Jewish and Polish history. He was influenced equally by a scholarly, religious father, who had a profound knowledge both of the Cabala and of modern philosophy, and by a beloved family servant, who took him with her to church and held fast to a ritualistic peasant Catholicism. Thus he grew up on a wavering line between Judaism and Christianity: an atheistic Jew with a skeptical intelligence and an underlying hunger for belief; a philosophical wunderkind (he was a Darwinist by the time he was six or seven years old) who simultaneously loved the Catholic liturgy and claimed ancestral descent from, among others, the eleventh-century Talmudist Solomon ben Isaac, Rashi of Troyes, and the well-known sixteenth-century Cabalist Isaac Luria. Nor did he forget that folk lullabies were his "first initiation into the thrill of metaphysics and into poetry." These contradictory early influences help to account for some of the anachronistic religiosity embedded in Wat's otherwise secular work, for the theological issues that, like Proustian memories, keep bubbling up to the surface of his poems.

Wat studied philosophy at the University of Warsaw and in some ways never recovered from his early reading of Schopenhauer, Kierkegaard, and Nietzsche. He had a philosophical cast of mind and a radical temperament—Mayakovsky called him "a born Futurist." Schopenhauer's bleak pessimism, Kierkegaard's idea of fear and trembling before an incomprehensible Absolute, Nietzsche's jubilant, unhappy proclamation that "God is dead"—these were for him gambits, first premises, philosophical beginnings. As a poet, Wat began by reacting against a cosmopolitan group of Polish poets forming around the magazine *Skamander*. The Skamandrites combined some qualities of the English Georgians and the Russian Acmeists. They were classical modernists who believed in biological vitalism and wrote skillful, mellifluous, optimistic, and metrically patterned lyrics that were on good terms with both the present and the traditional poetry of the past; their hearty first manifesto, reprinted in part in *The History of Polish Literature,* unequivocally declared, "We cannot hate the world, the earth is dear to us," and "We believe unshakably in the sanctity of a good rhyme, in the divine origin of rhythm, in revelation through images born in ecstasy and through shapes chiseled by work."

By contrast, Wat and his friends were barbarians at the gate who wanted to break down the rules and regulations of polite verse, to tear down the walls of form. They were Rimbaudian antipoets getting drunk on a new linguistic dynamism. Wat's first book, *Me from One Side and Me from the Other Side of My Pug-Iron Stove* (1920), is a quasi-Dadaist attempt to rupture diction and shatter syntax, to break the temporal lockstep of grammar, the cage of referential meaning. It is symbolism gone mad, words clumsily electrified and set free. Wat zealously embraced Marinetti's slogan "the liberated word"; he treated words as material things, as objects in and of themselves. Of course, Wat's shock tactics were a deliberate provocation not only to lovers of traditional Polish poetry—a horrified aunt accused him of "mutilating the beautiful Polish language"—but also to middle-class society itself. A scandalous manifesto of 1920 relegated civilization and culture to "the trash heap," abolished "history and posterity," ranted against "a social system dominated by genuine idiots," and looked forward to a time when "a pig will seem even more enchanting than a nightingale."

There is a strong sense in Wat's early work of romping through the graveyard of European civilization. His nihilism— his palpable catastrophic despair—culminated in the cynical stories of *Lucifer Unemployed* (1927), but as a poet he had already reached a modernist dead end, and he soon stopped writing. What happened to Wat between poetry books—between 1919 and 1957? He embraced a political fate, making a pact—what he eventually came to think of as an unholy alliance—with history itself. "Politics is our destiny," he wrote years later, "a cyclone in whose eye we constantly are even though we take shelter in the frail craft of poetry."

In *My Century,* Wat tracks and explores his spiritual history between the wars, documenting his literary and political experiences while searching for the meaning of what had happened not only to him but also to an entire generation of Central European intellectuals painstakingly broken on the wheel of totalitarianism. Wat's memoir returns time after time to what was unquestionably the central experience of his life: his voluntary, or "subjective," embrace of Communism. In the second half of the 1920s, Wat's despair gradually gave way to an all-encompassing ideology. He never joined the Party, but from 1929 to 1932 he edited the *Literary Monthly*. More than thirty years later he called the *Literary Monthly* "the corpus delicti of my degradation, the history of my degradation in communism, by communism." After the authorities closed the magazine, in 1932, Wat was arrested and spent several months in prison—a garden party compared with the Soviet jails he later inhabited—before becoming, despite his politics, the literary director of an influential Polish publishing house. The major transformation of his life, his full-scale education in suffering, began in earnest in 1939, when he fled from the German invasion of Poland to the zone occupied by the Soviet army. There he was subsequently arrested and accused of being a Trotskyite, a Zionist, even a Vatican agent. Temporarily separated from his wife and son, repeatedly interrogated, transferred from one Stalinist prison to another, abused, humiliated, evacuated, deported to various outlying Soviet cities, Wat underwent a profound spiritual conversion. He realized that he had been fundamentally wrong about Communism, about the true nature of evil, and about the role and function of poetry.

In prison, Wat came to believe in "the diabolical nature of Communism." It struck him with the force of a revelation, like a blow to the head, that a primitive demonism had been disguised as the great social experiment of his time. One night in Saratov Prison, Wat had a searing vision—probably induced by starvation—in which he saw a terrifying medieval devil with hooves, the figure of evil incarnate. All night its vulgar laughter approached and receded, until he began to suspect that the laughter of devilry was the sound of an anti-aircraft alarm from a boat patrolling the Volga. He interpreted this vision as a manifestation of history and of hatred and fanaticism, a piercing reminder that war had just broken out, a sign from the netherworld that Armageddon was approaching. But something in Wat shattered that night—some wall, some barrier—and thereafter he thought of himself as a religious hybrid: a Jew with a cross around his neck, a Christian with a Jewish intellect and conscience arguing with a menacing Old Testament God. His religious vision as well as his encyclopedic reading of history led him to conclude that evil is reincarnated in every epoch and that Bolshevism was "the devil in history," the twentieth-century embodiment of a metaphysical principle of the universe.

Wat's mystical experience humbled and transformed him. Reading his description of it is like hearing from a character in Dostoevski's late work updated for our century: a modern aesthete with a ferocious intellect and enormous learning remembers the night when he saw a primitive devil straight out of commonplace religious folk art. A watershed experience. Afterward, his attitude toward his cellmates changed. He joined prison society, thought less about himself, more about others. He became a fervent anti-leftist, coming to view Stalinism, and especially the "grandiose terror" of 1937 and 1941, not as an aberration but as the perfect logical culmination of Marxism-Leninism worked out in practice. It was the enemy of interiorization, of man's inner reality, a manifest reforging of souls, a "fanatic progressiveness" that in fact "excites and unleashes all of history's retrograde forces." In jail, Wat sounded the warning. He never forgave himself for his complicity in evil; indeed, he believed that he would have to go on paying with his own body forever. And slowly he began to recover his vocation as a poet.

In Lubyanka Prison, Wat rediscovered literature. Years later he wrote that he had hit rock bottom and that books had brought him back from despair, saving him from "the pendulum of prison time" that "swings between agony and nothingness" and immersing him in a world outside the cruel laboratory of prison life. He reexperienced literature as a process of "insight and synthesis." Reading Machiavelli, he encountered a "poet of action" who tempered his profound disgust with politics; rereading *Swann's Way*—a book in which "nothing had yet died but everything was dying"—he found a model for his agony in prison. Considering a Marxist critic's introduction to *Swann's Way*, which treated Proust as a "sociological trot," Wat decided that he was as strongly repelled by the way Communism flattened and reduced experience as he was by its atrocities. Lacerated by guilt and filled with self-hatred for his two or three years of "moral insanity," Wat began to think of poetry as spiritual consolation in the deepest sense, a purifying of demons. Tellingly, he compared the situation of the lyric poet with that of a prisoner who steps out of jail for a brief spell of writing; he called the poet "a wretched creature" who "struggles toward beauty from the abominable depths of his misery." Poetry became for him an ontological state; a way of associating and articulating phenomena; the imagination of a fallen creature in the presence of language. He considered himself a poet not simply because he wrote poetry (what he later called the "no-doubt-meaningless fact of writing verse") but because he struggled toward transcendence of our tragic fragmentation, because he had a radiant platonic dream of Being:

> But my life, oh, my life, had been a constant search for an enormous dream in which my fellow creatures and animals, plants, chimeras, stars, and minerals were in a pre-established harmony, a dream that is forgotten because it must be forgotten, and is sought desperately, and only sporadically does one find its tragic fragments in the warmth of a person, in some specific situation, a glance—in memory too, of course, in some specific pain, some moment. I loved that harmony with a passion; I loved it in voices, voices. And then, instead of harmony, there was nothing but scraps and tatters. And perhaps that alone is what it means to be a poet.

Thus Wat started to think of writing again. All his subsequent poems are, as he puts it, scraps and tatters; they are fragments and notes, the jagged remnants of a dream, or of a large, Rilkean quest. They are grief-stricken fallings away. The poet convicts himself of failure, remembers the loss. He said in a poem that he wrote in San Francisco near the end of his life:

> I, too, don't want to write the way I do. Would like it to be perfect,
> clear, sacral, as in Bach. And out of grief that I cannot,
> I am jotting down this poem as a grass snake imprisoned in a jar
> would write.

For Wat, the poet is a fractured being aspiring to a lost unity and wholeness, a guilty prisoner wounded by memory and longing for freedom.

Wat's six years as a prisoner and deportee in Russia changed him permanently. He and his family were reunited in 1942, and the ground for his poetic rebirth was essentially laid when he returned to Poland with them, in 1946. For three brief years he was once more active in the Polish literary world, but during the Stalinist era he was hounded and persecuted anew, forced to become a "non-person," to endure a protracted compulsory silence. In 1949, he had a debilitating stroke that almost killed him and from which he never entirely recovered. For the rest of his life, he suffered, somewhat mysteriously, from acute attacks of pain in his face and head. Wat himself believed that the terrible pain was a punishment for the "mortal sin" of being seduced by a totalitarian system; he declared outright that "the devil behind my illness is the devil behind communism." Yet after his stroke the Muse intermittently returned to him, and Wat was reborn as a poet. If his poems of the 1950s and 1960s are interrupted and uneven, they are also the flowers that have grown up out of the harsh soil of his illness. Wat committed suicide. His three late books—the poetry for which he will be remembered—constitute a small, unlikely, luminous night garden that survives his death.

In *With the Skin,* the odyssey of a Polish intellectual becomes the tormented wandering of a poet in exile. He has checked into too many neurological clinics and hotels. He finds himself drifting through the Alpine hills and recalling his nightmares on the shore of the Mediterranean; he considers the situation of a prostitute as he sits in a kitsch bar in a cheap section of Paris; he watches a chess game and listens to a heated conversation about metaphor and metonymy in a literary café in Berkeley. These locales are the stage settings or props for a work that has been fueled by displacement and dislocation, by flight, by fear and trembling. Wat's poetry, is, as Milosz argues, "all feeling and emotion, suffering." Its temperature runs high. Self-pitying and animated by guilt, filled with self-reproach and self-loathing (he never forgot that "there were among us those who sang for the strangers"), it is also comical and weirdly playful, self-mocking, simultaneously earnest and ironic. "Before Breughel the Elder" begins:

Work is a blessing,
I tell you that, I—a professional loafer!
Who bedded down in so many prisons! Fourteen!
And in so many hospitals! Ten! And innumerable hotels!
Work is a blessing.
How else could we deal with the lava of fratricidal love toward
    our fellow men?
With those storms of extermination of all by all?
With brutality that has no bottom, no measure?
With the black-and-white era which does not want to end,
endlessly repeating itself da capo like a record
forgotten on a turntable,
spinning by itself?

In Wat's world, consciousness is suffering, and "everything is equally unimportant, yes, unimportant / although so difficult, so inhumanly difficult, so painful!" Even death is "ineffective." Only work seems to provide a temporary release, a momentary rescue. The ancient maxim "Ora et labora" (Pray and work) ought to have been carved over the front door of Wat's house, if only he hadn't kept changing residences.

Exile is a permanent condition in Wat's poetry, a metaphysical state as well as a historical situation. Modern man is like the flamingo in his poem "A Flamingo's Dream," who begs the gods for land but instead finds "nothing except water." There is no rest, no stability. There is only the Baudelairean horror of living without end even as we hurtle toward annihilation. No wonder, then, that Wat envies the unchanging realm of stones, the "monastic rule and silence" of the mineral world. Stones are free from sequence and change, from intentionality, from eros and agape, from the process of decrepitude and disintegration, from guilt, from time. Unlike us, "they do not become, they are."

The specter of suffering, the memory of a medieval devil with hooves stealing unseen through the universe, the enormity of the catastrophe of our age, are never far from Wat's mind. Yet the very scale of the tragedy hampers and inhibits him, and he is seldom able to treat it directly. Rather, it shadows and glances across his work, emerging in parables and dreams, in sideways odes and letters, in a sly history lesson "From Hesiod," where the speaker claims that "Chthonic demons torture us" and laments that he was born in an era when the gods and the demigods had all disappeared. He cries out with biblical intensity:

Oh, why was I born in the time of their successors!
Once born, why didn't I die! Our time is of iron.
Our land is subject to a fierce invader,
our laws are shattered,
Nemesis abandoned us, forever,
violence and treachery sit on the throne
and there is no help in the deltas of rivers of desolation
in the iron age.

Wat's poems characteristically allude to rather than chronicle his own suffering. What happened to him, how his life was ruined by events—the way, as he put it, he stuck his little foot into History—forms the invisible backdrop, the unseen atmosphere of his work. It is the wind that pushes him, the secret air he breathes—untouched, omnipresent, what he is doomed to remember even as he tries to escape. In the eighth section of "Dreams from the Shore of the Mediterranean," he addresses himself and the subject of his disgrace as a haunted and harried man:

To the brim of memory
you are full of voices.
Voices from the house, voices from the garden, voices
from the forest, voices
from above you—they are gone and yet remain
and will not go away
even when the abortive human species disappears;
they will enter into
swallows, mosses, insects, stones, nothingness
if necessary. Into silence
which is the voice of the voice primeval.

How Wat longs to escape his conscience! But the voices follow him everywhere, even into the void. For him, everything living—consciousness itself—is a reminder of his own guilt-ridden hell, of "the heart's eternal sorrow."

Wat's poems are often structured around a journey—a long, haphazard walk, a metaphorical flight or descent. He is a belated Orpheus, destined to keep moving, longing for rest, envying the stillness:

> Disgusted by everything alive I withdrew into the stone world:
>   here
> I thought, liberated, I would observe from above, but
>   without pride, those things
> tangled in chaos.

Unlike the French poet Francis Ponge, who creates a phenomenology of the stone world in his prose poems, or Wat's countryman Zbigniew Herbert, who presents an objective aesthetic of that world in his pristine object poems, Wat, in the sequence "Songs of a Wanderer," struggles to enter entirely into the realm of the inert, into the heart and dreams of matter, to become "a stone among stones." In this he is close to the Theodore Roethke of the sequence "The Lost Son." But, whereas Roethke finds organic processes and archetypes for the human psyche in the natural world, Wat discovers only cold purity and silence, perfect stasis, liberation from time. "If God exists," Wat announces, "He is there. At the heart of stones." And He is inaccessible.

Wat's flight into the lower world is thwarted by a simple fact that he is still sealed up in a body, still living inside his senses. Just when he falls asleep and feels himself being transported into the "greater darkness" of the stone world, he is forced awake by the voices of the dead. They cry out *"Remember! Remember!"* even as they long to be forgotten, even as they seek oblivion:

>   Our hell—
> is in the memory of those who will survive us.
>   Driven out by the din and the sham
> of those whom I survived, I walked down through rubble. And
>   having lost
> everything I knew in that difficult descent, I am again what
> I had been.

Mutability and memory: there is no escape from the wheel of our fate.

"Ode III" is a powerful description of the poet's life inside his skin, an enactment of his bodily journey from innocence to experience, ecstasy to old age, joy to pain, Heaven to Hell. Whereas he once experienced "a Creation full of gifts" and believed in the holiness of the senses, in the youthful purity and joy of all that comes from the skin, he now discovers that his skin has become an instrument of imprisonment and shame, "a great, great misfortune," a cell. He is "grilled, lacerated, ploughed." His senses have conspired against him; the pain is infernal. "It is true, Hell has been promised to me long ago," he says, "but is not the promise being fulfilled too early?" At the conclusion of the poem the poet bequeaths his naked skin to his brethren to be tanned "for the binding of this collection of stanzas." He is martyred and views himself as a sacrificial beast who has been "dying without profit for a long, long, long time" and now lays down his body before the butcher's knife. He has wrested his work from the inner darkness; he has carved his poems out of himself. "Ode III" is an unflinching parable about the making of art in our century.

There is a ghostly internal struggle for objectivity in Wat's work. Existence is pain. The poet writes with the aim, usually unsuccessful, of outwitting suffering, of leaving behind something well made, objective, and consoling. This is an aspiration and a direction, mostly a failed dream. Wat's poems are steeped in subjective pain, yet in the ninth section of "Songs of a Wanderer" he cites Andrew Lang: "It is the nature of the highest objective art to be clean. The Muses are maidens." He follows this with one of the most redemptive moments in his poetry. For once the world seems washed in light:

> So beautiful the lungs
> are breathless. The hand remembers:
> I was a wing.
> Blue. The peaks in ruddy
> gold. Women of that land—
> small olives. On a spacious saucer
> wisps of smoke, houses, pastures, roads.
> Interlacing of roads, o holy diligence
> of man. How hot it is! That miracle
> of shade returns. A shepherd, sheep, a dog, a ram
> all in gilded bells. Olive trees
> in twisted benevolence. A cypress—their lone shepherd. A
>   village
> on a Cabris cliff, protected
> by its tiled roofs. And a church, its cypress and shepherd.
> Young day, young times, young world.

After all the clotted and claustrophobic suffering in Wat's work, it is enormously liberating to climb this mountain peak and breathe the fresh air of a perfect landscape.

In two stunning love poems to his wife, Wat picks up and dramatizes the idea of the maiden who must not be soiled. He praises, in the eleventh section of "Songs of a Wanderer"—a thirty-fifth anniversary poem—the sublimity of the family as one of "nature's creations" and marvels that "the tribe renews itself in the festoons of time":

> O, mountain streams
> Basalt beneath
> Bedrock of flight
> Pendulum-home
> Vise of the heart
> Lily of the soul
> Contralto of quiet
> And faithful shroud.
> Violet—sorrow,
> In winter flakes,
> O, you warm earth
> Of peaks and valleys!
> In sickness and in health
> Siamese sister
> My Bride.

In the final poem of the book, "The Bride," written five years later, for their fortieth anniversary, Wat treats the husband's approach to his wife, the bridegroom's to his bride, as an act of ritual purification. He asks to be cleansed and sanctified in order to be worthy of the beloved, to look upon and touch her. He speaks in the third person, and the love poem takes on the character of a Psalm, or of the Song of Songs:

> Let him not unveil her with his eye
> Before he washes it in the light
> Of morning, in the snows of a distant mountain,
> In a gentle hill of herbs,
> In the stream of the cantatas of Johann Sebastian
> Bach.

Let him not put his hand on her
Before he cleanses it of violence. From blood.
Spilled. Assented to. Before he engraves it
With tenderness, good deeds,
With the toil of laboring in earth the mother,
With playing a harpsichord or ocarina.

Let him not bring his lips closer to her
Before he rinses off the lie,
Before he drinks from the source of live water.
Before he burns them pure in live fire
Before he sanctifies them in the Tabernaculum
Of grace and sweetness.

A man who has been to Hell completes his life's work on a grace note of sweetness and light. In a way, all of Wat's work has been building toward just such a purifying fire. How long he has desired to rinse off the stain of history, to drink clean water, to recover a lost innocence, to touch the live flame and be released. And how far he has come on his journey to freedom.

There is no doubt that some of Wat's complexity is flattened out in English. Mr. Milosz notes that a good deal of Wat's linguistic playfulness is inevitably lost in translation, as are some of his lighter shades and tonalities, his verbal magic and inventiveness. There are no English equivalents for his coined words or sly transmutations of Polish grammar. And yet it is one of the mysteries of poetry, so notoriously untranslatable, that Wat's voice—witty, sardonic, impassioned—can reach us across the gulfs of language and experience; that an idiosyncratic Polish intellectual speaking from sunlit self-imposed exile in Italy and France, from the sealed prisonhouse of himself, can seem such an emblematic presence. I think we should read Aleksander Wat because his work is stark and uncompromising; because his poems go on talking late into the night; because his poetry flowered in pain and old age; because he made emotion primary and yet never relinquished his formidable intellect, his playfulness, or his wit; because he experienced the century with his body and wrote poetry with his skin; because he was relentlessly truthful and insisted on convicting himself; because his music began in Hell and quested for paradise; because he was a historical poet who wanted to be a metaphysical one; because he was inconsolable and never forgot his own destroyed world; because his poetry is a warning and a dream; because his intense suffering concluded on a radiant note of praise. Wat's poetic work is a tormented wandering through the day and the night. But now the odyssey is over; may the wanderer rest. He has embodied the truth of his own assertion: "Poetry fulfills itself when it is an act of heroism."

Wislawa Szymborska

Rapturous Skeptic

Wislawa Szymborska is Poland's foremost woman poet. She is also, along with Zbigniew Herbert and Tadeusz Rózewicz, one of the three major living Polish poets of her generation—all are significant European writers whose work spans the entire post-war period. Szymborska is less well-known in America than her European reputation warrants, perhaps, because she has always lived in Poland, where she has shunned the public eye and seldom commented on her own life or work. If Herbert, her better-known contemporary, is a figure comparable to, say, W. H. Auden, then Szymborska is roughly comparable to, say, Elizabeth Bishop—a writer for whom reticence seems to come naturally, whose modesty belies her literary ambitions, and who has quietly blossomed into a major twentieth-century poet. Yet Szymborska, like Herbert, has mounted a witty and tireless defense of individual subjectivity against collectivist thinking, and her poems, like his, are slyly subversive in the way they force us to reconsider received opinions. The rejection of dogma constitutes the basis of a canny personal ethics.

Szymborska was born in 1923 in the small town of Bnin in the Poznan area of western Poland. She moved with her family to Cracow when she was eight years old and has lived there ever since. She attended illegal school classes during the German occupation, studied Polish literature and sociology at Jagiellonian University after the war, and, from 1952 to 1981, worked on the editorial staff of the cultural weekly *Zycie Literackie* (*Literary*

Originally appeared as "Subversive Activities," in the *New York Review of Books,* 18 April 1996. Reprinted with permission from *New York Review of Books.* Copyright © 1996 NYREV, Inc.

Life). She has published nine individual collections of poems, several editions of her selected verse, and a volume of newspaper reviews and columns entitled *Lectury nadobowiazkowe* (*Recommended Reading*, 1973). She is also known to Polish readers as a distinguished translator of French poetry.

View with a Grain of Sand, translated by Stanislaw Barańczak and Clare Cavanagh (1995), brings together an even hundred poems spanning nearly forty years of Szymborska's work. It is by far the most extensive and readable edition of her poems yet to appear in English, though there have been three previous English-language translations: *Sounds, Feelings, Thoughts,* an excellent *en face* edition of seventy poems translated and introduced by Magnus J. Krynski and Robert A. Maguire (Princeton University Press, 1981); a *Selected Poems* that consists of forty lyrics translated by Grazyna Drabik, Austin Flint, and Sharon Olds (*Quarterly Review of Literature,* 1982); and *People on a Bridge,* a useful translation by Adam Czerniak (Forrest Books, 1990). Barańczak and Cavanagh have included nothing from Szymborska's first two books, *That's What We Live For* (1952) and *Questions Put to Myself* (1954) and only three poems from her transitional third collection, *Calling Out to Yeti* (1957). Her subsequent volumes are well represented: *Salt* (1962), *No End of Fun* (1967), *Could Have* (1972), *A Large Number* (1976), *The People on the Bridge* (1986), and *The End and the Beginning* (1993). Szymborska has always come through well in translation, through Barańczak and Cavanagh are the first to convey the full force of her scathing wit and startling imagination. They have reproduced the rhythm and rhyme schemes of some of her early poems, come up with deft equivalents for her wordplay, her neologisms, and her puns, and re-created the jaunty, precise, deceptively casual free verse style of her later work. My one complaint about this splendid book is that it comes without any supplementary information— it has no introduction, no commentary or notes, no afterword— and the reader who wants help with Szymborska's Polish references, or a sense of the biographical, linguistic, and political overtones of her work, has to look elsewhere.

Like others in her generation, Szymborska came of age during World War II and matured during a time when Stalinism dominated Polish political and cultural life. Thus did she see her country twice destroyed. She made her literary debut in

1945 with a poem in a Cracow newspaper and, by 1949, had her first volume scheduled for publication. The book hit a political snag, however, and never appeared. That same year Socialist Realism was hurriedly imposed on intellectuals by Party decree, and, in Czeslaw Milosz's summation, "the world of Orwell ceased to be a literary fiction in Poland." Szymborska's manuscript, which by all accounts combined a survivor's underlying guilt with a grievous sadness over her country's desecration, was attacked for being morbidly obsessed with the war and inaccessible to the masses—and therefore unpublishable in the Polish People's Republic.

The poets of Szymborska's generation responded to authoritarian pressures in different ways. Some, like Herbert and Miron Bialoszewski, chose internal exile, or "writing for the drawer"; others, like Rózewicz, who was already famous, and Szymborska, who was virtually unknown, decided to conform to the tenets of Socialist Realism. The poems that subsequently went into *That's What We Live For* (even the title is programmatic) and *Questions Put to Myself* (to a lesser extent) are filled with propaganda. They move from dogmatic denunciations of the old order to strident condemnations of Western imperialism, and they take the Party line on any number of subjects—from the Allied release of German war criminals to the Soviet position on the Korean War to the sufferings of working people under the capitalist system. A few of the love poems in *Questions Put to Myself* show a more reflective and inward bent, but the majority of poems on contemporary issues make discouraging reading. Propaganda didn't suit her sensibility very well—one critic described her style as "agitation-propaganda in a chamber-music manner"—and both these books are inferior to Szymborska's later work.

With her third collection, published after the "thaw" of 1956—the year that censorship famously loosened its grip in Poland—Szymborska began to sound her own note. It's hard to conclude much from the three poems that Barańczak and Cavanagh have included, but *Calling Out to Yeti* showed a fresh disillusion with Stalinist politics, revealing a mordant humor and skepticism. The figure of Yeti, the Abominable Snowman, is the book's central metaphor for Stalinism. Szymborska indicates that she did believe in Communism just as there were those who believed in the legendary snow creature from the north, but neither provided much human warmth or artistic comfort. Here is the conclusion to "Notes from a Nonexistent Himalayan Expedition":

> Yeti, we've got Shakespeare there.
> Yeti, we play solitaire
> and violin. At nightfall,
> we turn lights on, Yeti.
>
> Up here it's neither moon nor earth.
> Tears freeze.
> Oh Yeti, semi-moonman,
> turn back, think again!
>
> I called this to the Yeti
> inside four walls of avalanche,
> stomping my feet for warmth
> on the everlasting
> snow.

The snow here is very cold, very Siberian, but for the snow creature there would be no coming down to accommodate the vulnerability of actual human beings.

One of the best examples of Szymborska's new method is the opening poem, "Brueghel's Two Monkeys":

> This is what I see in my dreams about final exams:
> two monkeys, chained to the floor, sit on the windowsill,
> the sky behind them flutters,
> the sea is taking its bath.
>
> The exam is History of Mankind.
> I stammer and hedge.
>
> One monkey stares and listens with mocking disdain,
> the other seems to be dreaming away—
> but when it's clear I don't know what to say
> he prompts me with a gentle
> clicking of his chain.

Pieter Brueghel the Elder's painting *Two Monkeys in Chains* (1562) shows a pair of monkeys chained by the waist in the embrasure of a fortress wall. One is turned, the other turning away from the misty panorama of the city of Antwerp, which appears in the background. Brueghel's painting has been widely understood as a protest against the Spanish occupation of the Netherlands in the mid-sixteenth century. So, too, in 1957 Szymborska's poem was interpreted as a protest against the repressive Stalinist atmosphere that had so recently dominated Poland. The parallel—the political intonation—was unmistakable. The two monkeys—one filled with "mocking disdain," the other a daydreamer—are perhaps emblems of the poet's divided consciousness as she was forced to respond to the Stalinist historical test. Monkeys are also among Szymborska's favored creatures. Nervous, ironic, ugly—they are for her more humane than humans.

Szymborska hit her stride with her fourth book, *Salt,* and reached full maturity with *No End of Fun* and *Could Have.* Thereafter she hasn't so much developed as become ever more distinctly herself—a wry moralist balancing a capacity for creative wonder with a corrosive wit and an ironic historical awareness. "See how efficient it still is, / how it keeps itself in shape— / our century's hatred," she writes, and, "Our twentieth century was going to improve on the others":

> A couple of problems weren't going
> to come up anymore:
> hunger, for example,
> and war, and so forth.
>
> There was going to be respect
> for helpless people's helplessness,
> trust, that kind of stuff.
>
> Anyone who wanted to enjoy the world
> is now faced
> with a hopeless task.
>
> Stupidity isn't funny.
> Wisdom isn't gay.
> Hope
> isn't that young girl anymore,
> et cetera, alas.
>
> God was finally going to believe
> in a man both good and strong,
> but good and strong
> are still two different men.
>
> ("Our Century's Decline")

Szymborska's voice has the sting of long experience. It's as if each subject she takes up is first embraced but then undercut by her sharp, skeptical awareness.

Szymborska is an unusually conceptual poet, and her way of working is idiosyncratic, especially in her three most recent books: *A Large Number, The People on the Bridge* (perhaps her greatest single volume and one of the indispensable collections of Polish poetry in the 1980s), and *The End and the Beginning*. Reading great twentieth-century poets—Eliot, for example, or Vallejo—one feels the language moving mysteriously ahead of the thought, the combination of words unlocking perceptions deeper than the conscious mind—hence the high premium placed on the irrational and the unconscious in the creative process. In Szymborska's case the governing rationale of a poem takes precedence. She seems to begin with an abstract concept and then develop it in a variety of unexpected directions, quietly shifting to close range. Here is the poem "Could Have," which appears to be set in wartime Poland during the German occupation.

It could have happened.
It had to happen.
It happened earlier. Later.
Nearer. Farther off.
It happened, but not to you.

You were saved because you were the first.
You were saved because you were the last.
Alone. With others.
On the right. The left.
Because it was raining. Because of the shade.
Because the day was sunny.

You were in luck—there was a forest.
You were in luck—there were no trees.
You were in luck—a rake, a hook, a beam, a brake,
a jamb, a turn, a quarter inch, an instant.
You were in luck—just then a straw went floating by.

As a result, because, although, despite.
What would have happened if a hand, a foot,
within an inch, a hairsbreadth from
an unfortunate coincidence.

So you're here? Still dizzy from another dodge, close shave,
    reprieve?
One hole in the net and you slipped through?
I couldn't be more shocked or speechless.
Listen,
how your heart pounds inside me.

This lyric, which Krynski and Maguire translate as "There But for the Grace," may recall the tremendous uncertainty of the Nazi period with its sudden arbitrary arrests and deportations, but it is also about the radical contingency of experience itself, the absurd combination of things—the sheer dumb luck—that leads to anyone's survival. The speaker is marked by her awareness of the others—the unlucky, the singled out, the accident prone—who fell through the safety net. So, too, there is a sense of the vast distance between the world of things ("a rake, a hook, a beam, a brake . . .") and how much depends on them— survival itself. Even the most innocuous objects can seem like sinister wartime hazards. The ridiculous coincidences—the conditions—that lead to anyone's survival are hardly something to be proud of. It's as if we're all participating in an unrehearsed slapstick comedy. Hence the ironic shift to mock surprise at the end: "I couldn't be more shocked or speechless." The poem also takes a final plunge into the personal as the generalized you— your heart—comes to inhabit the speaker herself. She, too, has had her share of unwitting reprieves, which she pays for now with a guilty, rueful, incurable conscience.

Szymborska's mastery of the conditional gives an experimental feeling to much of her work. She likes to run through all the ramifications of an idea to see what it will yield; indeed, she has a gift for pursuing large, unanswerable questions with an off-handed charm and nonchalance. She typically begins with a simple paradoxical assertion—"The Great Mother has no face" ("A Paleolithic Fertility Fetish") or "Four billion people on the earth, / but my imagination is still the same" ("A Large Number")—which the poem breezily sets out to explore. Just as often a philosophical question is raised: can time be stopped by a work of art? ("The People on the Bridge"), is there an after-life? ("Elegaic Calculation"), and so forth. Because of her method, there's not much descriptive writing per se in her work

("Save me, sacred folly of description!" she cries out in "Clochard"), though she is capable of quick accurate brushstrokes. She has increasingly meditated on such huge general subjects as "Hatred" and "True Love," ranging from the mathematical concept of "pi" to the socialist ideal of Utopia to the joys of composing poetry. It's characteristic of her to write a poem rhetorically made up of questions ("Plotting with the Dead") or consisting entirely of apologies.

Here is the beginning of "Under One Small Star":

> My apologies to chance for calling it necessity.
> My apologies to necessity if I'm mistaken, after all.
> Please, don't be angry, happiness, that I take you as my due.
> May my dead be patient with the way my memories fade.
> My apologies to time for all the world I overlook each second.
> My apologies to past loves for thinking that the latest is the first.
> Forgive me, distant wars, for bringing flowers home.
> Forgive me, open wounds, for pricking my finger.
> I apologize for my record of minuets to those who cry from the
>   depths.

As this poem progresses, the speaker keeps shifting categories. She's filled with a wry sense of inadequacy as she begs forgiveness from inanimate objects as well as from emotions and concepts, from places as well as from groups of people, anthropomorphizing everything. There's a slightly bitter quality to the fact that everything has to be apologized to, nothing can be held in place for long. She finds herself narrowing the world to make it manageable, thereby trivializing it, and feels unequal to the world's constant sufferings and travails. All viewpoints are incomplete, all efforts inadequate: "My apologies to everything that I can't be everywhere at once. / My apologies to everyone that I can't be each woman and each man." The telling conclusion of this mini-epic is personal and stands as an encapsulated ars poetica:

> Don't bear me ill will, speech, that I borrow weighty words,
>   then labor heavily so that they may seem light.

Szymborska especially likes to play with scale and voice in her work. A favorite tactic is to take on a nonhuman perspective in order to expose what people are really like, letting a small animal like a tarsier talk, for example, or speaking from the point of view of a god examining human beings with an outraged, get-a-load-of-this attitude, as in "No End of Fun":

> So he's got to have happiness,
> he's got to have truth, too,
> he's got to have eternity—
> did you ever!

The speaker can't get over the sheer nerve of a creature who persists in carrying on in such a parochial fashion "with that ring in his nose, with that toga, that sweater." At times Szymborska can only bear human beings by looking at them from above, by removing herself enough to treat them as a subject of wild hilarity: "He's no end of fun, for all you say. / Poor little beggar. / A human, if we ever saw one." The miniaturization of human beings gives a Swiftian character to some of Szymborska's work. She vents her pessimism by shifting the scale to examine the human collective as if under a magnifying glass, the way a scientist might observe a colony of beetles. Satirical humor tipping over into dark cynicism is one way this poet expresses, and perhaps hedges against, recurrent despair.

Szymborska is a keen ironist of political cant ("We are children of our age, / it's a political age"), and she has a devastating way of using irony to attack sentimentality:

> And who's the little fellow in his itty-bitty robe?
> That's tiny baby Adolf, the Hitlers' little boy!
>   ("Hitler's First Photograph")

The key to Szymborska's style may well be the subversive sense of revision that animates her poems as she enters a debate already in progress or responds to a well-known story with a surprising perspective. For example, in "An Opinion on the Question of Pornography" she considers the issue of legalizing pornography from the standpoint of someone who immediately extends the argument to include all the scandalous pleasures of thought itself: "There's nothing more debauched than thinking," this speaker declares: "This sort of wantonness runs like a wind-borne weed / on a plot laid out for daisies." This poem should be understood in the context of the underground intellectual activities of the late 1970s (the time of the newborn oppositional movement) or the early 1980s (the martial law period), when people gathered in private apartments to study forbidden books. Sometimes the secret police parked outside to intimidate participants in this orgy of thinking. The poem is filled with playful double entendres ("It's shocking, the positions, / the unchecked simplicity with which / one mind contrives to fertilize another!"), but also has a sinister undertone:

> Only now and then does somebody get up,
> go to the window,
> and through a crack in the curtains
> take a peep out at the street.

Stupidity isn't funny anymore, especially when it's aligned with power and thinking is considered dangerous to the state.

Szymborska's revisionary sensibility is well displayed in one of her most daring poems, "Lot's Wife," which retells the familiar biblical story from the vantage point of the main character. The poem rapidly shifts from the general to the particular, immediately complicating our sense of motive and perspective, setting off a chain reaction:

> They say I looked back out of curiosity,
> but I could have had other reasons.
> I looked back mourning my silver bowl.
> Carelessly, while tying my sandal strap.
> So I wouldn't have to keep staring at the righteous nape
> of my husband Lot's neck.
> From the sudden conviction that if I dropped dead
> he wouldn't so much as hesitate.
> From the disobedience of the meek.
> Checking for pursuers.
> Struck by the silence, hoping God had changed his mind.

"Lot's Wife" is a quickly spiraling catalogue of possible reasons why she might plausibly have turned back. It's alert to what might motivate an actual woman to defy an injunction from God and permanently seal her fate. The details are so specific that the idea she turned back out of simple "curiosity" comes to seem pallid and vague, concealing more than it reveals. Each detail forces us to picture a person actually leaving her home. Yet each reason also displaces the others, so that we can't reliably tell whether Lot's wife turned back from torpor or desolation, shame or loss. It may be too psychologically complicated even for her to comprehend and unravel ("I looked back for all the reasons above"); in fact, it all may have been a huge inadvertence ("I looked back involuntarily"). Szymborska has probed the story with an intimacy that permanently transforms it. Despite its playful sense of psychological possibilities, however, the poem still enacts a woman's bitter fate:

> No, no. I ran on,
> I crept, I flew upward
> until darkness fell from the heavens
> and with it scorching gravel and dead birds.
> I couldn't breathe and spun around and around.
> Anyone who saw me must have thought I was dancing.
> It's not inconceivable that my eyes were open.
> It's possible I fell facing the city.

In Szymborska's work we're always on the edge of an abyss, imperiled, in a comical situation or evading close shaves in a world where death claims the right of way. It's not only accidents we have to contend with but a brutal historical record, more deaths than we can count, hatred that never tires of its favorite leitmotif ("the impeccable executioner / towering over its soiled victim"), catastrophes that defy the imagination. Yet the realist also notes that the world keeps mysteriously renewing itself, even on battlefields. This is the framing theme of "Reality Demands":

> Reality demands
> that we also mention this:
> Life goes on.
> It continues at Cannae and Borodino,
> at Kasovo Polje and Guernica.
>
> There's a gas station
> on a little square in Jericho,
> and wet paint
> on park benches in Biba Hora.

Letters fly back and forth
between Pearl Harbor and Hastings,
a moving van passes
beneath the eye of the lion at Cheronea,
and the blooming orchards near Verdun
cannot escape
the approaching atmospheric front.

There's so much Everything
that Nothing is hidden quite nicely.

Eventually, even the worst destructions recede, and pure being reasserts itself. Comedy prevails over tragedy: "On tragic mountain passes / the wind rips hats from unwitting heads / and we can't help / laughing at that."

Szymborska's bitterness about human fallibility and forgetfulness mingles with her sense of the world's unfathomable richness. Time and again she finds herself revitalized by commonplace miracles, by what one poem terms "miracle fair": fluttering white doves, a small cloud upstaging the moon, mild winds turning gusty in a hard storm, the inescapable earth. Yet she also chafes against the rule-bound natural world, necessity's confines. In a poem about evolution slyly entitled "Thomas Mann," she writes: "Dear mermaids, it was bound to happen. / Beloved fauns and honorable angels, / evolution has emphatically cast you out." But what evolution eventually rejects the poet's imagination can still accept, and she exults that Mother Nature never anticipated a creature like the German novelist: "she somehow missed the moment when a mammal turned up / with its hand miraculously feathered by a fountain pen." In one of her signature poems, "The Joy of Writing," Szymborska playfully investigates the nature—and the process—of the poetic imagination itself. Here the author puzzles over what she has just written—"Why does this written doe bound through these written woods?"—and contemplates the way words repeatedly blossom into things. The final three lines create a triple equivalence: "The joy of writing. / The power of preserving. / Revenge of a mortal hand." What is so arresting is the sudden shift from joy to power to revenge. Writing becomes a form of protest against the incontestable ravages of time. The poet takes vengeance on mortality by thinking the unthinkable and presiding over her own creation.

Szymborska is a cool-eyed skeptic who keeps returning to the way the world defies and evades the names we give it, and she never forgets that we exist in the midst of a universe we can't comprehend. That's why "View with a Grain of Sand" is an appropriate title poem for this volume.

> We call it a grain of sand
> but it calls itself neither grain nor sand.
> It does just fine without a name,
> whether general, particular,
> permanent, passing,
> incorrect, or apt.

Repeatedly shifting perspective, Szymborska's poetry embraces the modernist position that all views are partial and restricted, all truths relative. These poems make us more rather than less uncertain of the names we impose on things. "My identifying features / are rapture and despair," she writes, and she has become one of the finest poets in contemporary Europe by pitting her dizzying sense of the world's transient splendor against unbearable historical knowledge.

Philip Larkin
Sour Majesty

Philip Larkin has increasingly come to seem the greatest English poet after W. H. Auden, though the word *great* is perhaps mildly inapplicable to a writer of such slender output and narrow range. Yet he was, as Auden himself said in a fiftieth-birthday tribute, "a master of English language," a poet whose near-perfect phrasing, emotional honesty and directness, and clarity of artistic purpose permanently stamped his generation. Larkin essentially wrote from personal experience, his verbal antennae precisely attuned to unhappiness—"happiness writes white," he said, quoting the French novelist Montherlant. He understood poetry as "emotional in nature and theatrical in operation," and his carefully honed style combined a self-deprecating, razorlike wit with an unshakable sense of worldly disappointment, of desires unfulfilled and dreams thwarted. His famous remark to an interviewer that "deprivation is for me what daffodils were for Wordsworth" is both funny and acute since the misery of diminished and unfulfilled experience is his enduring subject. Indeed, it is difficult to think of him as young—this man who seemed to have been born middle-aged, regretting a past that never took place and terrified of oncoming death. The tone of sour majesty, of sardonic resignation infused with wordless romantic yearning, is something we might call Larkinesque.

During his lifetime Larkin became one of the best-loved English poets, a reclusive figure at the heart of the English sensibility. His formidable reputation basically rests on three thin, irreplaceable volumes whose combined contents come to eighty-five poems: *The Less Deceived* (1955), which made his mark and

From the *Wilson Quarterly* (summer 1993).

established his voice; *The Whitsun Weddings* (1964), which made him famous in England ("It turned his voice into one of the means by which his country recognized itself," his biographer Andrew Motion writes); and *High Windows* (1974), which converted him into something of an English national treasure and made him internationally known. These were gathered together and chronologically rearranged in Anthony Thwaite's edition of the *Collected Poems* (1988), which also includes Larkin's early poems, written from his teens up to the publication of his first book, *The North Ship* (1945), as well as previously unpublished and uncollected lyrics. The arrangement dilutes Larkin's scrupulous effects and well-ordered individual collections, but it also gives a fuller sense of the writer at work, his clustering themes and chronological development. Larkin's' bibliography also contains two early novels, *Jill* (1946) and *A Girl in Winter* (1947), written in his early twenties (his first overriding ambition was to be a novelist), and two nonfiction miscellanies, *All What Jazz: A Record Diary, 1961–1971* (rev. ed. 1985) and *Required Writing: Miscellaneous Pieces, 1955–1982* (1983). Larkin's reputation was further enhanced by the controversial success of his edition of *The Oxford Book of Twentieth-Century English Verse* (1973), which succeeded Yeat's *Oxford Book of Modern Verse* (1936). Larkin's edition gave canonical authority to his traditional poetic values and anti-Modernist tastes, his commitment to formal poetry written for a general readership. The voice of disillusion was also a conserver of English traditions.

After the death of his friend Sir John Betjeman in 1984, Larkin was generally expected to become the next poet laureate of England. The rumor persists that he was passed over because of the profanity in his work satirizing family values ("They fuck you up, your mum and dad"), but in truth he was offered the position by Mrs. Thatcher and turned it down. Larkin always refused to be in any way publicly involved with poetry. (He once said about poetry readings, "I don't want to go around pretending to be me.") He found appearing in public an ordeal, jealously guarded his privacy, and suffered what would turn out to be a near-terminal writer's block. ("Poetry has deserted me," he was already complaining in 1967.) He thought the laureateship had become "show-biz" and was not surprised when Ted Hughes, whose work he disliked, accepted the position. But if Hughes, a romantic primitivist who glories in preindustrial Albion, became the official laureate, then Larkin remained until his death, as Donald Davie suggested, "the effective unofficial laureate of post-1945 England." Davie observed that "we recognize in Larkin's poems the seasons of present-day England, but we recognize also the seasons of an English soul."

Larkin drew a thick curtain between his private life and his public persona. He dismissed his childhood in the smallish Midlands city of Coventry as "a forgotten boredom" and encouraged the notion that nothing had ever happened to him. At Oxford during the war years ("Oxford terrified me," he admitted later) he wrote both poetry and prose and was associated with the generation of Kingsley Amis and John Wain. Afterward, he worked as a librarian in Wellington, Leicester, and Belfast before settling down at the University of Hull. For the last thirty years of his life he cultivated his disguise as an ordinary person—a working chap, a bachelor, a middle-brow. "Whatever a poet is supposed to look like, it's not me," he said typically. He was, by all accounts, unfailingly courteous, bald and bespectacled and increasingly deaf, formal in a dark suit and tie ("death-suited"), stern but amiable, quiet and shy, but also droll and at times wickedly funny. He obviously took a great deal of pleasure in expressing himself as Philip Larkin, in his own playful articulate refusals and his unyielding posture of bleakness. He liked turning his dislike of things into a spectacle for his friends and delighted in comic exaggerations. "To say that he had a sense of humor," the novelist A. N. Wilson cautioned about Larkin's antic humor, "would be to imply that he sometimes said things which it was safe to take wholly seriously."

Not many detected the level of rage that seethed inside him. Larkin never hid his negative opinions of others, but he parceled them out and displayed them with a witty tact. In *Required Writing*, for example, one encounters his offhanded sense of other people ("Everyone envies everyone else"), his commitment to bachelorhood ("I see life more as an affair of solitude diversified by company than as an affair of company diversified by solitude"), his distaste for children ("Until I grew up I thought I hated everybody, but when I grew up I realized it was just children I didn't like"), his ideas about being abroad ("I wouldn't mind seeing China if I could come back the same day"), and his conservative political views ("I adore Mrs. Thatcher"). He was right-wing and said, "I identify the Right with certain virtues and the Left with certain vices." He was also a monarchist and one of his last poems, dated March 2, 1978, is a quatrain written to commemorate the Queen's Jubilee. He called it "a lapidary lark":

> In times when nothing stood
> but worsened, or grew strange,
> there was one constant good:
> she did not change.

The poem is now inscribed on a memorial stone in Queen's Square garden.

Larkin believed that "the impulse to preserve lies at the bottom of any art," and many of his poems preserve the memory of a fading England. "Never such innocence / Never before or since," he writes in his hymn to old England, "MCMXIV." In a sense Larkin's mature tone settles down into a knowing acceptance of Englishness, of what it means to be English. The poem "The Importance of Elsewhere," which he wrote after living in Belfast for five years, begins, "Lonely in Ireland, since it was not home, / Strangeness made sense," and concludes:

> Living in England has no such excuse:
> These are my customs and establishments
> It would be much more serious to refuse.
> Here no elsewhere underwrites my existence.

There is a Larkin of cricket and English seaside holidays, of country churchyards, native coastlines, and small market towns. But he catches the country at a point where it is endangered, hemmed in on all sides, on the verge of disappearing. The stately cadences of "Going, Going" are explicit:

> And that will be England gone,
> The shadows, the meadows, the lanes,
> The guildhalls, the carved choirs.
> There'll be books; it will linger on
> In galleries; but all that remains
> For us will be concrete and tyres.

Larkin's England is an Edwardian pastoral that has been dese-crated by a relentless encroaching modernism ("greeds / And garbage are too thick-strewn / To be swept up now"). It is a provincial glory, besieged and vanishing.

Larkin's anxiety about the social and political developments of the 1960s was directly expressed in such satirical poems as "Naturally the Foundation Will Bear Your Expenses," "Take One Home for the Kiddies," and "Homage to a Government," which takes up the subject of Britain's withdrawal from a domi-nant military role on the world stage. "Homage" publicly articu-lates what Larkin told Barbara Pym privately—that he was "deeply humiliated at living in a country that spends more on education than on defense." Here is the last stanza:

> Next year we shall be living in a country
> That brought its soldiers home for lack of money.
> The statues will be standing in the same
> Tree-muffled squares, and look nearly the same.
> Our children will not know it's a different country.
> All we can hope to leave them now is money.

The sadness associated with Britain's loss of power is not just a personal neurosis; it reflects the pessimism of Larkin's class facing its reduced place in the world. Larkin is not usually such an overtly political poet; rather, he presents himself as a lyricist of dwindled prospects, of leaves falling away from their trees and seasons fading, of people being pushed to the side of their own lives. But the politics associated with Larkin's personal sad-ness are encoded in his work since his autumnal feelings of disappointment continually point to a national feeling of cul-tural decline and decreased imperial power. Larkin was the unofficial laureate of a gray, postimperial, postwar England.

He cultivated a stellar, anti-intellectual pose as one of the lesser deceived. Larkin made no secret of his anticosmopoli-tanism, his anti-Americanism, his hatred of "the aberration of Modernism, that blighted all the arts." He took every opportunity to whack the Modernist giants (Pablo Picasso, Ezra Pound, Char-lie Parker). He also made much of his literary conversion from Yeats to Hardy, which he defined as a rejection of grand rhetori-cal gestures and an acceptance of human limits. Hardy gave him confidence in his own authoritative pessimism. Thereafter Larkin always insisted on an empirical, antiheroic, antitranscendental poetic. He took a skeptical, commonsensical approach to poetry, ridiculed anything that smacked of "literature," and pretended to be a nonreader. One of his best-known poems, "A Study of Reading Habits," concludes, "Books are a load of crap." Or, as he told an inquisitive interviewer, "I read everything except philosophy, theology, economics, sociology, science, or anything to do with the wonders of nature, anything to do with technology—have I said politics?"

Of course this is absurd coming from a university librarian. The pose is belied both by the quality of Larkin's writing—you don't get to write the way Larkin did without being an acute reader—and by the sly, mostly buried range of references in his work, especially to French Symbolism. In another format he admitted, "I've always been a compulsive reader," and acknowledged keeping twelve poetic exemplars within reach of his working chair: Thomas Hardy, William Wordsworth, Christina Rossetti, Gerard Manley Hopkins, Siegfried Sassoon, Edward Thomas, William Barnes, Winthrop Praed, John Betjeman, Walt Whitman (!), Robert Frost, and Wilfred Owen. Many of Larkin's opinions seemed part of an elaborate put-on, a vast private joke. Yet there was also a truth expressed in Larkin's stance against reading that may, after all, suggest an anxiety about the "unmanliness" of literary activity. As his work progressed, he increasingly fenced off more and more of the outside world, eventually excluding other people's thoughts and ideas entirely, dispensing with other people's passions by filing them away according to the Dewey decimal system.

This past year, however, a "national treasure" became, to judge by the ferocious debates in the English press, a national problem. The carefully erected barrier between Larkin's private life and his public persona was breached by the publication of two books by his literary executors: Anthony Thwaite's voluminous edition of the *Selected Letters of Philip Larkin,* which contains over seven hundred letters to more than fifty recipients, and Andrew Motion's judicious biographical account, *Philip Larkin: A Writer's Life.* In England the *Letters* appeared first and the biography afterward; in the United States the process has been mercifully reversed. Late in his life Larkin reviewed lives of

Auden and Cecil Day-Lewis and declared he was "rather depressed by the remorseless scrutiny of one's private affairs that seems to be the fate of the newly dead. Really, one should burn everything." That "remorseless scrutiny" has now turned in his direction. Larkin was constitutionally unable to burn anything himself—he was as ambivalent about this as about almost everything else—but on his deathbed he instructed his longtime companion, Monica Jones, to destroy the thirty-odd thick volumes of his diary, which she subsequently did. The rest of his papers survived, and the damage is profound.

The publication of Larkin's *Letters* created a controversy in England that will go on echoing for years. Almost all of the discussion has focused on the most repellent aspects of the correspondence: Larkin's racism, his xenophobia, his misogyny. It is as if he had exposed the sewer of the English soul. Certainly that is not what the editor of these *Letters* had intended. "What is remarkable," Anthony Thwaite writes in his tactful, somewhat hopeful introduction , "is how consistently Larkin emerges, whoever he is writing to. Books, poems, jazz, cricket, drink, the daily grind of 'the toad, work,' exasperation with colleagues and friends, gossip about them, depression at the state of the world and of himself, concern with whatever concerned the person to whom he was writing, occasional delights in the occasional delight he experienced—all are here, in the vividly speaking voice of someone who, even when he was joking, told the truth as he saw it." After this mild description, it is a shock to turn to the often foul-mouthed letters themselves. These letters, especially the ones to his male cronies Kingsley Amis, Robert Conquest, and Colin Gunner, were a time bomb that has now exploded. Many readers suspected Larkin's prejudices all along—his attitudes kept seeping into his poems, reviews, and interviews—but not many were aware of the virulence with which they were privately expressed. What began as a set of grim jokes and biases slowly hardened into a catalogue of intense hatreds. Larkin never pretended he enjoyed being Larkin—"Life is first boredom, then fear," he summarized in "Dockery and Son"—but the *Letters* indicate the depth of his self-absorption and self-disgust, his ever-deepening misery and despair, his rancid view of other people.

Many of the letters are uncontroversial. There is an exemplary, well-known correspondence with Barbara Pym—one of the few writers he truly admired—and a friendly series of letters to his editors at Faber and Faber, in particular Charles Monteith. There are youthful, exuberant letters to his schoolmates in which he talks about his ambition to be a novelist, his early enthusiasm for Auden and Lawrence, his devotion to jazz. He writes chatty letters to female friends, carries on a savvy business correspondence relating to his poems, and writes warmly to other writers who are promoting his work. But Larkin's misanthropy is always lingering and gives a decided cast to the correspondence. "Bugger everything & everybody," he says. His scorn begins at home. Near the end of his life he calls himself "a pregnant salmon" and describes his "sagging face" as "an egg sculpted in lard, with goggles on." "I hated myself so much I was trying to disappear altogether," he jokes in italics at the bottom of one letter. "So now we face 1982," he confesses in another, "gargantuanly paunched, helplessly addicted to alcohol, 'tired of livin' and scared of dyin', world famous unable to write poet."

Larkin's self-disgust quickly spilled over to others, and not many escaped his bile. He especially mocked anyone connected to literature. "I have a huge contempt for all 'groups' that listen to and discuss poetry," he wrote. In his characterizations Emily Dickinson becomes "Emily Prick-in-son," the poets David Jones "a farting prick" and W. D. Snodgrass "a dopy kid-mad sod." The critic H. E. Bates becomes "H. E. Bastard," and in a splenetic catalogue Larkin asks, "When will these soding loudmouthed cunting shiftstuffed pisswashed sons of poxed-up bitches learn that there is something greater than *literature*?" Nor are Larkin's friends exempt. Anthony Powell was taken aback to find himself described as a "creep" and a "horse-faced dwarf." About Kingsley Amis, to whom he is permanently linked, Larkin says, "The only reason I hope to predecease him is that I'd find it next to impossible to say anything nice about him at his memorial service."

The letters show that Larkin's poetics of preservation were countered by an equal need to mock and denigrate. Hence the lifelong undergraduate prank that he shared with Amis of signing off with the word *bum* at the end of letters: "Man that is born of woman hath but a short time to bum," "The Tories may lose the election owing to Mrs. Thatcher's bum," and so forth. Larkin moves easily from irreverently joking about individuals to lacerating groups. He calls the Irish "driveling slack-jawed blackguards" and exclaims, "What dreary no-good cunts these foreigners are." His racism is especially repellent. He advises Amis to "keep up the cracks about niggers and wogs"; he speaks of "fat Caribbean germs pattering after me in the Underground." He announces, "And as for those black scum kicking up a din on the boundary—a squad of South African police would have sorted them out to my satisfaction." Here is a little ditty on "How to Win the Next Election" that he sent to Conquest, Gunner, and Monteith:

> Prison for strikers,
> Bring back the cat,
> Kick out the niggers—
> How about that?

Larkin's letters sometimes make a spectacle of being offensive, at least partially for the shock effect—"Ooh, Larkin," he feigns, "I'm sorry to find you holding these views"—but that makes his opinions no more funny or palatable.

Here is the "unwritten" Jubilee poem to Her Majesty that Larkin sent to Thwaite:

> After Healey's trading figures,
> After Wilson's squalid crew,
> And the rising tide of niggers—
> What a treat to look at you!

This is the "unofficial" quatrain buried under the "official" one, the political undertow, the racist joke that should be inscribed on the backside of the stone in Queen's Square garden. The shadow side of Larkin's right-wing politics was a fury against everything Other: Jews, blacks, women, immigrants, academics, trade unions. He despised everything and everybody, especially himself.

The letters are only the tip of the iceberg. "Please believe me," Larkin told an adolescent friend, "when I say that half my days are spent in black, surging, twitching, boiling HATE!!!" It is no longer possible to discount this aspect of Larkin's character, which was so inextricably tied to his creativity. His wretchedness was extreme. Apparently, the letters are mild in comparison to the diaries. The evidence suggests, as Andrew Motion says, that "even his most candid letters only hint at their intensity." The one person who glimpsed some of the diaries, his friend Patsy Strang, reported that they were sexual logbooks ("very masturbatory") and, in Motion's characterization, "a gigantic repository for bile, resentment, envy, and misanthropy." Larkin may have hated the Modernists, but he had more in common with them than he supposed. He now takes his place in a line of reactionary twentieth-century writers—from Yeats, Pound, and Eliot to D. H. Lawrence and Wyndham Lewis—whose lives (and works) were fueled by repulsive right-wing hatreds. But what was for an earlier generation a rising tide of democracy and leveling modern values was for Larkin a flood that had already taken place. He has just about drowned. His defense, in "This Be The Verse," was a tone of sardonic chuckling, a grim, half-comic misery:

> Man hands on misery to man.
> It deepens like a coastal shelf.
> Get out as early as you can,
> And don't have any kids yourself.

Motion's biography is helpful in deciphering the clues to Larkin's character and in creating a context for his opinions. Larkin led an outwardly uneventful life—he was so self-divided and focused on writing that he mostly kept from doing anything—but a secretive, tumultuous inner life. He thrived off his own refusals and flourished on his own pessimisms. Motion locates Larkin's problems somewhere among his repressed homosexuality (never acknowledged), his latent anti-Semitism (which scarcely figures into the correspondence), and the definitive influence of his parents, especially his beloved father, who was a prewar Nazi sympathizer. Far from forgetting his childhood in Coventry, Larkin remembered it all too well. He never recovered from his parents' cramped, loveless marriage, a "bloody hell" he vowed never to repeat. He seemed to have combined something of his mother's excruciating timidity (as a child he was nearsighted and stammered badly) with his father's authoritarianism, thus trapping himself between opposing impulses. Larkin always attributed his negative feelings about travel ("filthy abroad," he called it in the *Letters*) to two trips he took to Germany with his father.

Motion acutely speculates on the ambivalence and shame Larkin must have felt—"embarrassment at best, humiliation at worst"—about being in Germany in the late 1930s. By the late 1920s Larkin's father had already become, as one acquaintance said, "an active and impenitent admirer of Germany's postwar recovery, and of Hitler's role in achieving this." Larkin vehemently denied his father was a fascist, acknowledging that Sydney Larkin was "the sort of person democracy didn't suit." Larkin sometimes mocked his father's opinions, but, as Motion notes, he "never actually disagreed with him—never sympathizing with the suffering of others, and sometimes even making a few mildly anti-Semitic and pro-German remarks of his own." Larkin's anti-Semitism surfaces in his late poem "Posterity," where his satirically named biographer, Jake Balokowksy, laments:

"I'm stuck with this old fart at least a year;

I wanted to teach school in Tel Aviv,
But Myra's folks"—he makes the money sign—
"Insisted I got tenure."

Larkin's anti-Semitism is rarely this overt, but his attitude toward the Jew as the despised Other magnetized many of his other hatreds.

Larkin also picked up many of his father's negative opinions about women. He had little or no contact with girls during his childhood and adolescence, and prejudice replaced knowledge. Women became for him remote and unimaginable. They sent him, as he confessed to his schoolmate James Sutton, "rigid with fright." Larkin's sexual anxiety and diffidence soon turned to sneering: "Women (university) repel me inconceivably," he told Sutton. "They are shits." "FUCK ALL WOMEN!" he writes elsewhere. "I am quite fed up with the whole business . . . Sex is designed for people who like overcoming obstacles. I don't like overcoming obstacles." Those obstacles were mostly insurmountable and lifelong, since Larkin's personality exquisitely balanced sexual attraction with sexual revulsion. Motion narrates the story—or nonstory—of Larkin's handful of stalled love affairs, especially with Monica Jones and Maeve Brennan ("Yes, life is pretty grey up in Hull," he wrote to Robert Conquest in

1966, "Maeve wants to marry me, Monica wants to chuck me"). His contradictory feelings left him at a permanent standstill.

Larkin thought of marriage as a "revolting institution," and his intense physical and emotional needs were countered by an equally intense fear of connection and commitment. He was convinced women used sex to snare men into marriage, which he thought of in the most conventional domestic terms. In the cartoonish situation of "Self's the Man," for example, poor, emasculated Arnold is run ragged because of his "selflessness":

> He married a woman to stop her getting away
> Now she's there all day,
>
> And the money he gets for wasting his life on work
> She takes as her perk
> To pay for the kiddies' clobber and the drier
> And the electric fire,
>
> And when he finishes supper
> Planning to have a read at the evening paper
> It's *Put a screw in this wall*—
> He has no time at all . . .

Revolted by the idea of family responsibilities, Larkin also felt victimized by his own desires and often turned to pornography for consolation. The fact that his letters carry on a steady stream of casual, pornographic, and misogynistic remarks obfuscates but does not obliterate his sexual frustration and alienation, his sexual envy, bewilderment, and fear. It was largely because of his feelings about women that he came to define life as "an immobile, locked, / Three-handed struggle between / Your wants, the world's for you, and (worse) / The unbeatable slow machine / That brings what you'll get" ("The Life with a Hole in It"). Women became for him symptomatic of the life he would never lead, the incarnation of unfulfilled, unfulfillable desires.

Larkin's sexual conflicts were repeatedly played out in his work, from the earliest poems in *The North Ship* to his final lyrics. In "Reasons for Attendance" he opposes "the wonderful feel of girls" to his own solitary calling to "that lifted, rough-tongued bell / (Art, if you like)." The problem was that he was still beset and bewildered by his own desires, terrorized by a solitude he had chosen but could not entirely tolerate ("Only the young can be alone freely," he concludes in "Vers de Société") and desperately needed to defend. He felt victimized for having chosen "a life / Reprehensibly perfect" ("Poetry of Departures"). Hence the bitter resentment of the first stanza of "The Life with a Hole in It":

> When I throw back my head and howl
> People (women mostly) say
> *But you've always done what you want,*
> *You always get your own way*
> —A perfectly vile and foul
> Inversion of all that's been.
> What the old ratbags mean
> Is I've never done what I don't.

Larkin's work charts the forms of his deprivation in terms of women: the turmoil of losing the girl, of desiring the beautiful girl he cannot have and not desiring the unattractive, problematic one he might get, of being too middle-aged for the sexual revolution. Larkin is known as a great poet of mortality, of aging and death, but, as his biographer suggests, "Reading his poems in chronological sequence, it is clear that his obsession with death is inextricable from his fascination with love and marriage." What Motion calls "fascination" is more accurately described as fascinated revulsion.

The specter of the white male poet turning reactionary in later life is hard to face and even harder to think about clearly. What are the implications? English poetry is not inevitably aligned with reactionary politics—one thinks of Byron and Shelley—and there is no reason that lyric sadness and disappointment cannot be linked to a democratic and progressive social action. It is rare but possible. In Larkin's case, however, as in many others, the poet's narcissistic wounds found outlet in a hierarchical politics of exclusion. It is not sufficient to say, as the *London Times* did, that "what matters about Larkin is the handful of melancholy and funny poems that captured the mood of his times." The problem is that Larkin's attitudes, now made explicit in the *Letters* and biography, are shot through his work. They are not "accidental" or merely unworthy of him. They shadow his poems like an unwelcome aura. They are stitched there like threads that we suspected were present all along and now can see. Naturally, this affects our unraveling of his work. Larkin's need to preserve was balanced by an equally intense desire to desecrate, and hatred was the flip side of his gloomy tenderness. "What will survive of us is love," he wrote in "An Arundel Tomb," but rage was the underbelly of his art.

Larkin's late personal lyrics show us the world from the point of view of someone who feels that love has been completely withdrawn from him. Hatred is one reaction to that withdrawal, an ugly solace and refuge in a place where privation reigns. He feels cheated and blames others for his misery; he is imprisoned with his own inexcusable desires. Rather than expressing blame directly, the poems tend to celebrate and exacerbate the wound of lovelessness. Larkin's poems are not introspective. They do not lead him to "greater understanding." They are clenched, acerbic, unforgettable—the voice of bitterness itself. They are brokenhearted and utterly perfect and defensively armored. At times, they are irresistibly funny and highly quotable, and many readers have found themselves reciting them from memory. Their lyric melancholy, splendid phrasing, and corrosive brilliance are like a magnet to poetry readers. But what is being magnetized? The poems move from the wry irony of "Annus Mirabilis"—

> Sexual intercourse began
> In nineteen sixty-three
> (Which was rather late for me)—
> Between the end of the *Chatterley* ban
> And the Beatles' first LP.

to the grander resentment of "Sad Steps"—

> a reminder of the strength and pain
> Of being young: that it can't come again,
> But is for others undiminished somewhere.

to the putrefying envy and jealousy of "Love Again"—

> Someone else feeling her breasts and cunt,
> Someone else drowned in that lash-wide stare,
> And me supposed to be ignorant,
> Or find it funny, or not care,
> Even . . . but why put it into words?

Here the voyeuristic fury turns to helplessness and then to frustrated silence. By the end of his life's work Larkin's world had been hopelessly reduced; all that was left was the open sore of lovelessness and the prospect of "unresting death," endless oblivion.

Larkin made no secret of his final bafflement and dread. It was all he had left, his concluding weapon. He despised other people but could not bear to be alone ("Vers de Société"); he was disgusted by "the whole hideous inverted childhood" of aging ("The Old Fools"); he felt his mind going blank from the blinding glare of death, "not in remorse," he said, for "the good not done, the love not given," but at the thought of total emptiness, "the sure extinction that we travel to / And shall be lost in always" ("Aubade"). He went on complaining but knew that complaints wouldn't save him ("Death is no different whined at than withstood"); he raged against others but knew that rage devoured itself. He had found his last wretched place in an unloved, unlovable universe. His viewpoint narrowed further and further until in the end all that remained of the heart's knowledge was a clear lens for viewing unacceptable death:

> Where has it gone, the lifetime?
> Search me. What's left is drear.
> Unchilded and unwifed, I'm
> Able to view that clear:
> So final. And so near.
>
> ("The View")

The view into oblivion was so chillingly personal, painful, and direct that ultimately the poet wanted only to obliterate it. He longed for oblivion itself, an end to the old wound, the agony of consciousness:

> It will be worth it, if in the end I manage
> To blank out whatever it is that is doing the damage.
>
> Then there will be nothing I know.
> My mind will fold into itself, like fields, like snow.
>
> ("The Winter Palace")

This poem is dated November 1, 1978, and it is no surprise to discover that from then on the mind folding back entirely into itself would not be able to sustain more than a handful of occasional lyrics. There was nothing left for it in poetry. Resentment had run dry.

It is altogether remarkable then to turn back to a poem such as "High Windows" and find the same self-damaging rage transfigured, the same constellation of feelings remade. The unrelieved arc and movement of this poem, with its crafty mix of dictions and characteristically ironized longings, is Larkin at his artistic peak. It moves from a sardonic and profane bitterness about sex and religion to a final wordless perception of high windows:

> When I see a couple of kids
> And guess he's fucking her and she's
> Taking pills or wearing a diaphragm,
> I know this is paradise
>
> Everyone old has dreamed of all their lives—
> Bonds and gestures pushed to one side
> Like an outdated combine harvester,
> And everyone young going down the long slide
>
> To happiness, endlessly. I wonder if
> Anyone looked at me, forty years back,
> And thought, *That'll be the life;*
> *No God any more, or sweating in the dark*
>
> *About hell and that, or having to hide*
> *What you think of the priest. He*
> *And his lot will all go down the long slide*
> *Like free bloody birds.* And immediately
>
> Rather than words comes the thought of high windows:
> The sun-comprehending glass,
> And beyond it, the deep blue air, that shows
> Nothing, and is nowhere, and is endless.

The visionary clairvoyance at the end of this poem points to an eternal realm, a Pascalian emptiness beyond the confines of language. It is rapturous and terrifying and free. "High Windows" reminds us that art exists beyond biography, that Larkin, too, was a vehicle for his feelings, that the sourness of his life could also be transformed into the spirit's majesty.

Derek Walcott

"Either I'm Nobody or I'm a Nation"

"There is a force of exultation, a celebration of luck, when a writer finds himself a witness to the early morning of a culture that is defining itself, branch by branch, leaf by leaf, in that self-defining dawn," Derek Walcott says in his Nobel Prize lecture for 1992. That force of exultation and celebration of luck, along with a sense of benediction and obligation, a continuous effort of memory and excavation, and a "frightening duty" to "a fresh language and a fresh people," have defined Walcott's project for the past four and a half decades. He has always been a poet of great verbal resources and skills engaged in a complex struggle to render his native Caribbean culture: the New World—not Eden but a successor to Eden, a polyglot place, an archipelago determined to survive—a world he calls "a ferment without a history, like heaven . . . a writer's heaven."

Derek Walcott is the greatest poet and playwright writing in English that the West Indies has produced. His *Collected Poems* (1986) is in itself a massive achievement, bringing together work from ten previous books written between 1948 and 1984. It moves from his first privately printed pamphlet, *Twenty-five Poems,* to his Lowellian sequence *Midsummer.* It includes early work from *In a Green Night: Poems 1948–1960;* middle work from *The Castaway, The Gulf,* and his major autobiographical poem *Another Life* (which is his *Portrait of the Artist as a Young Man*); and

"Derek Walcott: 'Either I'm Nobody or I'm a Nation' " was commissioned by and appeared originally in a special issue of the *Georgia Review* (spring 1995) on the Nobel Laureates in Literature. Copyright © 1995 by the University of Georgia. Reprinted by permission of the *Georgia Review.*

later work from *Sea Grapes, The Star-Apple Kingdom,* and *The Fortunate Traveller.* Since the *Collected Poems* he has published *The Arkansas Testament* (1987) and *Omeros* (1990), the latter a book-length reprise to *The Odyssey* that parallels Greek and Antillean experience and stands as the capstone of his poetry thus far. The themes of Walcott's poems are echoed and counterpointed by the late ritual action and colloquial language of his major plays, from *Dream on Monkey Mountain* to *Remembrance* and *Pantomine* and on to *Beef, No Chicken, The Last Carnival,* and *A Branch of the Blue Nile.* Reading through Walcott's lifework one is always aware of the covenant he has made with a people and a place.

Walcott has repeatedly sought to give voice to the inlets and beaches, the hills, promontories, and mountains, of his native country. His birthplace of St. Lucia is one of the four Windward Islands in the eastern Caribbean, a small craggy place that faces the Atlantic Ocean on one side and the Caribbean Sea on the other. The sea—or what he has called "the theatre of the sea"— is an inescapable presence in his work and has fundamentally affected his sense of being an islander, a poet of a floating new world surrounded by water. "The sea was my privilege / And a fresh people," he writes in *Omeros,* where he also defines the ocean as "an epic where every line was erased // yet freshly written in sheets of exploding surf." At the same time, Walcott has been a determined advocate of pan-Caribbean literature and culture, considering each island an integral piece of one larger historical unit. He thus defines himself as part of a constellation of writers—among them St.-John Perse, Aimé Césaire, and C. L. R. James—who have created one literature in several different languages, and he belongs to a generation who have often described their sense of excitement and creative possession at writing about places for the first time, defining their role in terms of what Alejo Carpentier calls "Adam's task of giving things their names."

Walcott is a writer who exults in nouns and verbs, in the tang of vernacular speech, in the salty, sea-drenched sound of words themselves. He has one of the finest ears of any poet writing in English since Hart Crane or Dylan Thomas. It is as if the very vowels and consonants of his vocabulary had been saturated in the sea ("When I write / this poem, each phrase go be soaked in salt," the seaman-poet Shabine declares in "The Schooner *Flight.*") Here is the beginning of the early lyric "A Sea-Chantey":

> Anguilla, Adina,
> Antigua, Canelles,
> Andreauille, all the *l's*
> Voyelles, of the liquid Antilles . . .

There is a quality of earthly prayer in the way Walcott luxuriates in sounds and savors letters, turning over the words, holding up the names. A sacred sense of vocation informs his high eloquence and powerful commitment to articulating his native realm, calling out "the litany of islands, / The rosary of archipelagoes" and "the amen of clam waters." As he puts it in "Another Life":

> The Church upheld the Word, but this new Word
> was here, attainable
> to my own hand,
> in the deep country it found the natural man,
> generous, rooted.

Walcott's early work was inspired by a deep sense of privilege and opportunity, a fundamental feeling that he was speaking not just out of his own experience but also from everything he saw around him, naming a world thus far undefined:

> Forty years gone, in my island childhood, I felt that
> the gift of poetry had made me one of the chosen,
> that all experience was kindling to the fire of the Muse.
> ("Midsummer")

Walcott has always been attracted to writing "soaked in salt," testing the richness of his own linguistic impulses against the simple clarities of the natural world, seeking a transparent and gritty style "crisp as sand, clear as sunlight, / Cold as the curled wave, ordinary / As a tumbler of island water" ("Islands"). He grew up speaking English, English patois, and French patois, but in his early work he mostly bifurcated those languages, mining the resources of English in his poems and exploring the possibilities of patois in his plays. In such groundbreaking dramatic works as *The Sea at Dauphin, Ti-Jean and His Brothers,* and *Malcochon,* he used a Creole-inflected language, still a mostly uncharted territory for West Indian literature, and turned outward to render the landscape and life of West Indian foresters and fishermen.

The language of Walcott's boyhood bubbles to the surface in his autobiographical work *Another Life,* which fixes in place his childhood and youth in St. Lucia and tells the story of the growth of a poet's mind, of how "he fell in love with art, / and life began." There is also a key moment in *Sea Grapes* when he brings his multiple linguistic heritages together in his poems. (Significantly, *Sea Grapes* is the first book to contain a large number of poems about being away from the West Indies.) The moment takes place in the poem "Sainte Lucie," a lyric infused with homesickness, when the speaker suddenly cries out, "Come back to me / my language," and calls up the French patois of his childhood: "C'est la moi sorti," he says, "is there that I born." Thereafter, Walcott has often imported dialect into his poetry. He has called himself "a mulatto of style" (a phrase borrowed from Senghor) and explored the different registers of speech in a series of dramatic monologues as well as in his epic poem *Omeros.* And he has thereby given a place in his poems to the contending languages—contending cultures—at work inside him. The Odyssean figure of Shabine undoubtedly speaks for his creator when he uses the demotic and turns the language of colonial scorn into a source of pride:

> I'm just a red nigger who love the sea,
> I had a sound colonial education,
> I have Dutch, nigger, and English in me,
> and either I'm nobody, or I'm a nation . . .

One way to view Walcott's work is as an energizing struggle to reconcile a divided heritage. His pact with his island, his first commitment to describing the world around him, was balanced by a sense of self-division and estrangement. He grew up as a "divided child"—a Methodist in an overwhelmingly Catholic place, a developing artist with a middle-class background and a mixed African, English, and Dutch ancestry, coming of age in a mostly black world, a backwater of poverty. Some of the dramatic tension in his work comes from the gap he has always had to cross to describe the people with whom he shared an island. At the same time, his "sound colonial education" was accompanied by a rueful awareness that "the dream of reason / had produced its monster: / a prodigy of the wrong age and colour." In a sense Walcott's real work began with his dual commitment to the English literary tradition and to the untouched country he wanted to re-create in his writing. From the beginning he was faced with the precocious burden of his choices, pulled between mimicry and originality, between the Old and New Worlds.

Walcott has described himself at nineteen as "an elated, exuberant poet madly in love with English," and says that he saw himself as "legitimately prolonging the mighty line of Marlowe, of Milton." With no vital Caribbean literary tradition to draw upon, he turned for models to the English metaphysicals and to such poets as T. S. Eliot and W. H. Auden. He was so gifted an assimilator that by the time of his first major collection, *In a Green Night,* Robert Graves could say, "Derek Walcott handles English with a closer understanding of its inner magic than most (if any) of his English-born contemporaries." Something of the cost of Walcott's British influence, however, is reflected in the anguished questions that conclude his most famous early poem, "A Far Cry from Africa":

> I who am poisoned with the blood of both,
> Where shall I turn, divided to the vein?
> I who have cursed
> The drunken officer of British rule, how choose
> Between this Africa and the British tongue I love?
> Betray them both, or give back what they give?
> How can I face such slaughter and be cool?
> How can I turn from Africa and live?

Over the course of his career Walcott has implicitly answered these questions by increasingly affiliating himself with a line of New World poets, with writers from the Americas who had stood for a syncretism of cultures and an accompanying New World aesthetic. "Mongrel as I am, something prickles in me when I see the word 'Ashanti' as with the word 'Warwickshire,' " Walcott has said, "both separately intimating my grandfathers' roots, both baptising this neither proud nor ashamed bastard, this hybrid, this West Indian." The task for the hybrid Antillean artist is to fuse the diverse fragments, to piece together the African, Asiatic, and European shards into a new whole by rejoicing in the ferment and the babel, glorying in the bricolage of West Indian culture.

A great deal of rage—an invective—sometimes breaks loose in Walcott's work as a fury against racism: against those who have typed the poet as neither white nor black enough ("The first chain my hands and apologize 'History,' " Shabine says, "the next said I wasn't black enough for their pride"); against those who still view the Caribbean people as illegitimate and rootless ("There are no people there," the pamphleteer Froude wrote, "in the true sense of the word"); against the legacies of slavery and colonialism and "the incurable sore / of poverty"; against a venal middle class "who want a new art / and their artists dying in the old way"; against the "ministers of culture, ministers of development" who sold out the idea of a federation and have been eager to prostitute West Indian culture ("Adam had an idea. / He and the snake would share / the loss of Eden for a profit. / So both made the New World. And it looked good"). Shabine expresses this overwhelming rage when he warns

> . . . all you best dread the day I am healed
> of being a human. All you fate in my hand,
> ministers, businessmen, Shabine have you, friend,
> I shall scatter your lives like a handful of sand,
> I who have no weapon but poetry and
> the lances of palms and the sea's shining shield!

Faced with such a devouring anger and bitter alienation, Walcott has often turned to the splendors of a "a virginal, unpainted world" shining beyond the claims of history or politics. And he has kept in mind his abiding covenant. When Shabine anchors in Castries harbor in St. Lucia, he can say with quiet pride:

> I have kept my own
> promise, to leave you the one thing I own,
> you whom I loved first: my poetry.

The Adamic task is finally a healing one, since the poet overcomes history and turns back with reverence to his first realm.

Throughout his work Walcott has delineated the enigmas, paradoxes, and dilemmas of the Antillean artist trying to shoulder—and shoulder aside—the burdens of a colonial heritage. Robinson Crusoe was his first, and indeed his most persistent, symbolic figure for the West Indian artist. In his early and middle work Walcott returned often to the Crusoe story ("our first book, our profane genesis") because it represented for him the double nature of working out one's destiny on a small island. Walcott's Crusoe despairs at being shipwrecked and alone—the very titles of *The Castaway* and *The Gulf* suggest the burdens of artistic isolation—but he is also exhilarated at being the monarch of his island. He is Adamic man, the "first inhabitant of a second paradise," a resilient chronicler of an unspoiled surrounding. Crusoe also enacts the process of colonization, since he saves Friday but then transforms him into a servile figure. The poet himself is both Crusoe and Friday, a castaway forging the tools for a new culture.

The figure of the castaway has slowly shifted in Walcott's work to the figure of the exile, the wayward but fortunate traveler. "I accept my function / as a colonial upstart at the end of an empire," he says wryly in the poem "North and South," "a single, circling, homeless satellite." In each of his books since *Sea Grapes* Walcott has written poems set in both the Caribbean and abroad, moving between cultures, setting up a dialogue between the emblematic "North" (metropolitan countries) and "South" (the Caribbean). *The Fortunate Traveller,* for example, has three sections: "North," "South" and "North"; *The Arkansas Testament* is divided into two parts, "Here" (St. Lucia, the Caribbean, the anchor "home") and *Elsewhere* (which stands for all other foreign landscapes but most especially America and the American South). His increasing cosmopolitanism and range, expressing a global vision of empire, have been accompanied by an equivalent restlessness, a greater feeling of distance from his origins. Throughout his life Walcott has written poems of painful self-awareness and homecoming, among them "Homecoming: Anse la Raye," "Return to D'Ennery, Rain," the final chapter of *Another Life,* "The Lighthouse," and "The Light of the World." These take up the subject of how far he has grown from his provincial past, of "homecomings without home." The fear that he has abandoned the people around him ("I, who could never solidify my shadow / to be one of their shadows") becomes the prelude to a renewed commitment to the making of an Antillean art.

Walcott's recent stage version of *The Odyssey* is especially appropriate, since the figure of the exile in his work has slowly bled into the character of Odysseus, a wandering Everyman on a roundabout journey home. Walcott's observation at the beginning of *Sea Grapes* is characteristic:

> That sail which leans on light,
> tired of islands,
> a schooner beating up the Caribbean
>
> for home, could be Odysseus,
> home-bound on the Aegean . . .

All of Walcott's personae—his various fortunate travelers, returning spoilers, and mulatto seamen—are Odyssean types. Shabine's travels in "The Schooner *Flight*" are a veritable Odyssey, and when he declares, "Either I'm nobody, or I'm a nation," he is echoing that moment in the Greek epic when Odysseus slyly deceives the Cyclops by calling himself "Nobody." He is also asserting that this "nobody" is the culture's representative figure, "a nation." As Walcott's exiles have turned into Odyssean figures, so his tutelary poetic spirit has become Homer. The pattern of Homeric imagery in his work culminates in *Omeros,* which is the Greek name for Homer, the archetypal singer of tales.

Omeros is a poem of epic scope. It doesn't deal with the supernatural deeds of gods or demigods ("Forget the gods and read the rest," Omeros tells the narrator), and it doesn't try to ennoble the people it is about, but it does try to tell the tale of a tribe, to give voice to "the whole experience of the people of the Caribbean." Omeros is both a character in the book and a prototype of the artist as castaway—a kind of Robinson Crusoe—singing about the earth's poor, lost and dispossessed. He is a Protean figure who appears as the blind man "Seven Seas," a vagrant in London, an Indian shaman, the American artist of the sea Winslow Homer, and the Virgilian guide leading the narrator through the inferno of history. The Antillean people appear in the poem with Homeric names (Achille, Hector,

Philoctete, Helen), and the poem ranges across a wide array of historical events, taking up the genocide of Native Americans, the tragedies of African enslavement, the horrors of World War II, the isolated suffering of individuals in exile. "I sang our wide country, the Caribbean Sea," the narrator says, and behind the poem is the idea that the sea itself contains the memories of all those who perished in it. The Homeric bard unearths the lost lives and shattered histories, but he also sings of a new people and a new hope.

Walcott is ultimately a poet of affirmations, a writer who believes that the task of art is to transcend history and rename the world. As he says in "The Antilles: Fragments of Epic Memory": "For every poet it is always morning in the world. History a forgotten, insomniac night; History and elemental awe are always our early beginning, because the fate of poetry is to fall in love with the world, in spite of History." In the end and the beginning, the poet's enterprise is a redemptive one, a joyous calling. Derek Walcott's lifework is a grand testament to the visionary powers of language and to the freshening wonders of a world that is always starting over again despite History, a world that is always startling and new.

Yehuda Amichai

Poet at the Window

1

For more than thirty years Yehuda Amichai has been conducting his own highly personal war on forgetfulness and silence. He has the unique ability to render and enact the complex fate of the modern Israeli, the individual man locked in and responding to history. Amichai is a historical poet of the first order, a political writer in the deepest sense of that term. At the same time, he is a writer who always speaks of his own concerns, his private love pangs and personal questions, his parents' history and his own intimate secrets. Part of the achievement of Amichai's work has been the conjoining of these two spheres, always speaking of one in terms of the other. Indeed, one of the central themes of his work has been the way the personal is implicated in the historical, the private impinged upon by the public. Always his poems register the human implications of the political event—in Lorca's phrase, the drop of blood that stands behind the statistics. In a way, the poet is like one of Emerson's "representative men" transferred to Jerusalem and updated for the second half of the twentieth century, a prophet who shuns the traditional role and speaks in the guise of an ordinary Jewish citizen concerned with his people and his place. He is, like Wordsworth, a passionate man trying to speak to other men, and, as a modern Hebrew poet, his work is appropriately steeped in the common imagery of the Prayer Book and the Psalms, the communal imagery and

This essay expands on a piece of the same title that first appeared in the *American Poetry Review* 10, no. 3 (1981).

mythology of the Hebrew Bible, the underground stream of Jewish mysticism.

Most often Amichai speaks without the mask of a fictive persona, as an individual witness, a quiet man who is always standing at the window. The poem "Out of Three or Four in a Room" (from *Poems,* translated by Assia Gutmann) captures and enacts precisely what it means to be a witness, a writer trying to bridge the speechless and enormous distance between the inadequate and false words (cut loose and "wandering without luggage") and the terrible event. It is a poem that in the example of its making transcends its own pessimism, but it shows too that, as Williams said, "There is nothing sacred about literature, it is damned from one end to the other."

Out of Three or Four in a Room

Out of three or four in a room
One is always standing at the window.
Forced to see the injustice amongst the thorns,
The fires on the hill.

And people who left whole
Are brought back in the evening, like small change.

Out of three or four in a room
One is always standing at the window.
Hair dark above his thoughts.
Behind him, the words.
And in front of him the words, wandering, without luggage.
Hearts without provision, prophecies without water
And big stones put there
And staying, closed, like letters
With no address; and no one to receive them.

Amichai is a poet who may say truthfully that "I go out to all my wars." He was born in Wurzbürg, Germany, in 1924 and immigrated with his parents to Palestine in 1936. He fought with the British army in World War II and then in three Israeli wars—in 1948, 1956, and 1973. He speaks from experience when he talks of children "growing up half in the ethics of their fathers / and half in the science of war" (from *Selected Poetry,* translated by Chana Bloch and Stephen Mitchell). One of the shocks that gave rise to Amichai's poetry was the confrontation between the protected world of his childhood (a world of sweet parental love and strict religious observance) and the hard actualities of adult life. As Chana Bloch suggests in her foreword to the *Selected Poetry,* he has spent his entire adulthood in the midst of Israel's struggle at first to exist, then to survive. He has not escaped that difficult history, or what he calls "the complicated mess" of Israeli life. The poem "Like the Inner Wall of a House" reports that

> I found myself
> Suddenly, and too early in life
> Like the inner wall of a house
> Which has become an outside wall after wars and devastations.

Wars and devastations are behind all of Amichai's work. Sometimes the knowledge of war is implicit in his poems, in their background of sadness, terror, and loss—but just as often it is imminent and explicit, violently affecting him. And the place where they impinge most is on his own love life, for Amichai is perhaps first and foremost a love poet, a writer preeminently concerned with the tenderness and ironies of sexual love. And he is continually waking to find that love engulfed by the external historical world. He writes, "In the middle of this century we turned to each other," thus specifying the personal moment in terms of the larger epoch, and he announces wryly that:

> Even my loves are measured by wars:
> I am saying this happened after the Second
> World War. We met a day before the
> Six-Day War. I'll never say
> before the peace '45–'48 or during
> the peace '56–'67.

In his perceptive introduction to *Amen* (1977), Ted Hughes comments on the way in which Amichai's imagery ramifies both outwards and inwards, wedding the private to the public. Hughes writes:

> Writing about his most private love pangs in terms of war, politics, and religion he is inevitably writing about war, politics, and

religion in terms of his most private love pangs. And the large issues are in no way diminished in this exchange . . . Each poem is like a telephone switchboard—the images operate lightning confrontations between waiting realities, a comic or terrible conversation between the heavy political and spiritual matters and the lovers.

Perhaps the finest example of Amichai's conjunction of love and politics (or love and war, or love and religion), his imagistic tangle of supposedly separate but inevitably tangled realms, is the poem "A Pity. We Were Such a Good Invention" (also from *Poems*). This poem is remarkable for its directness and profound simplicity, its unique mixture of the erotic and the political, its subtle tone of outrage and nostalgia. As a love poem, it is worthy to stand beside "The River Merchant's Wife: A Letter" or, more appropriately, "The Good-Morrow" and "The Canonization." The Amichai of the 1950s and 1960s was a somewhat formal and metaphysical poet, a tender ironist influenced by W. H. Auden (especially in his conjunction of the private and the political spheres) and George Herbert (mainly in his redefinition of the metaphysical conceit); John Donne was an especially strong early influence, and this poem has some of the qualities, though presented retrospectively, of "For God's sake hold your tongue, and let me love . . ." It reads:

A Pity. We Were Such a Good Invention

They amputated
Your thighs off my hips.
As far as I'm concerned
They are all surgeons. All of them.

They dismantled us
Each from the other.
As far as I'm concerned
They are all engineers. All of them.

A pity. We were such a good
And loving invention.
An airplane made from a man and wife.
Wings and everything.
We hovered a little above this earth.

We even flew a little.

The final memory of this poem, understated and passionate, may be effectively placed against the violent and surgical destruction of the unspecified "them." Here the lovers are not "stiffe twin compasses," as in Donne's famous image, but, appropriate to their century, "an airplane made from a man and wife." There is a sad, ironic, outraged, bitter, and wistful tone in the homely invention of this little hovering aircraft. And, though it is true that there is an enormous burden in this act of remembering, there is also a vehement anger and determination. This is the same poet who will convincingly title another poem "To Remember Is a Kind of Hope." Because to remember *is* a kind of hope, particularly as those hopes are embodied in poems.

2

Amen begins not at the window but in the street, and it starts out not with the poet but with Mr. Beringer, "whose son / fell by the Canal." Mr. Beringer is the first of many in this book who has lost a son or a husband or a father or a lover. He is grief-stricken and responsible to his dead son, and because of the weight of that responsibility (or rather because of the weight he is losing) the poet becomes responsible to him.

> Mr. Beringer, whose son
> fell by the Canal, which
> was dug by strangers
> for ships to pass through the desert,
> is passing me at the Jaffe gate:
>
> He has become very thin; has lost
> his son's weight.
> Therefore he is floating lightly
> through the alleys,
> getting entangled in my heart
> like driftwood.

The poem, "Seven Laments for the Fallen in the War," goes on to speak of the monument to the unknown soldier, which, ironically and because it is on the enemy's side, will become "a good target marker for the gunners / of future wars." It remembers

Dicky, who was hit "like the water tower at Yad Mordecai"; there "everything poured out of him." It speaks of "Bitter salt . . . dressed up / as a little girl with flowers" and a dead soldier who "swims above little heads / with the swimming movements of the dead." These laments come from a country where "everything [is] in three languages: Hebrew, Arabic, and Death." He asks the heartfelt question, "Is all of this sorrow?" The answer: yes.

> "May ye find consolation in the building
> of the homeland." But how long
> can you go on building the homeland
> and not fall behind in the terrible
> three-sided race
> between consolation and building and death?

And in this world even an old textbook, faulty but tender-hearted, becomes an emblem of a friend who died "in my arms and in his blood."

> I found an old textbook of animals,
> Brehm, second volume, birds:
> Description, in sweet language, of the lives
> of crows, swallows and jays. A lot of mistakes
> in Gothic printing, but a lot of love: "Our
> feathered friends," "emigrate to warmer
> countries," "nest, dotted egg, soft plumage,
> the nightingale," "prophets of spring,"
> The Red-Breasted Robin.
>
> Year of printing 1913, Germany
> on the eve of the war which became
> the eve of all my wars.
>
> My good friend, who died in my arms and in his blood
> in the sands of Ashdod, 1948, in June.
>
> Oh, my friend,
> red-breasted.

One of the remarkable and metaphysical aspects of this sly and sad poem is the way the feelings for the textbook imply, without becoming sentimental, the tender feelings for the friend. The connection is made with lightning-like precision, the name of the robin transformed and infused with new meaning as it comes to represent the dead soldier, frozen in time, red-breasted. And by speaking about this outdated textbook of animals ("year of printing 1913") the poet lines the poem not only with sorrow, but with warmth and affection too. Indeed, the sixth lament makes this distinction important: "Yes, all this is sorrow" . . . but leave / a little love burning, always / as in a sleeping baby's room a little bulb." The lightbulb gives off "a feeling of security and silent love" that keeps us from giving ourselves wholly to grief. It is true that sometimes, as on Memorial Day in the seventh lament, the poem itself gives way, mixing grief with grief, sorrow with sorrow, until the poet (in "camouflage clothes of the living") cries out, much as one imagines Job crying out:

> Oh, sweet world soaked, like bread,
> in sweet milk for the terrible toothless God.

In these poems Amichai's sardonic Jewish quarrel with God reaches a fever pitch worthy of the biblical prophets. "We begged / for the knowledge of good and evil," he complains to the Lord in another poem, "and you gave us / all kinds of rules like the rules of soccer" (*Selected Poems*). But against this, and with a terrible irony infusing a kind of tender hopefulness, the poem juxtaposes its final line: "Behind all this some great happiness is hiding."

Amichai's war poems are unique in that they are informed by a strong sense of personal responsibility—the self simultaneously implicated in and victimized by the war—or, as one poem puts it, "the hunter and the hunted in one body." No poem demonstrates this sense of personal responsibility, the individual voice assuming the weight and burden of these collective deaths (and what is that collective but a sum of individuals?) better than the fourth poem in "Poems from a Cycle Called 'Patriotic Songs.' " The poem begins, typically, with a disclaimer about itself ("I have nothing to say about the war"), and it ends, also typically, with a complex and sweet-voiced affirmation.

> I have nothing to say about the war,
> nothing to add. I'm ashamed.

All the knowledge I have absorbed in my life
I give up, like a desert
which has given up all water.
Names I never thought I would forget
I'm forgetting.

And because of the war, I say again,
for the sake of a last and simple sweetness:
The sun is circling round the earth. Yes.
The earth is flat, like a lost, floating board. Yes.
God is in heaven. Yes.

This final affirmation, in a language that is itself a kind of last and simple sweetness, is particularly poignant in that it is an affirmation of a world that has long been lost, a world that has been initiated into another kind of knowledge. The extraordinary sense of a world that has a flat wooden surface and a calm God can only predate 1913, that dark eve of all our wars, when the West put on its helmet of fire and, like the Hebrew poet, "crossed the borders of being an orphan." It is now a blood-stained, red-breasted world for adults, and, as an early poem of Amichai makes clear, "God takes pity on kindergarten children . . . but adults he pities not at all."

He abandons them,
And sometimes they have to crawl on all fours
In the roasting sand
To reach the dressing station
And they are streaming with blood.

(*Poems*)

It is with this knowledge and through these eyes that one must consider Amichai's final affirmation. Somehow and all at once that affirmation is simultaneously sincere and ironic, terribly honest and tender, deceptively simple and impossible. Perhaps most of all it is impossible. And yet, like Rilke in his self-portrait, the poem does make its affirmation, "it says its yes."

Reading Amichai's poems is a harrowing experience. The sheer accumulated weight of these losses is enormous. I find it nearly impossible to read these poems, however successful, as a merely literary performance. Their human presence is too close. Even the weakest poems, and some of the little love poems toward the end of the book seem tossed off and merely cute, bear a particular stamp. Ultimately, these poems may not have the stature of, say, Whitman's poems, but, as in Whitman, one cannot read them without simultaneously touching the man who stands behind them. At times, in their deepest moments, in their naked splendor, the simple recital of losses may take on the quality of a sacred litany. Here is Amichai's eleventh "Patriotic Song."

> The town I was born in was destroyed by shells.
> The ship in which I sailed to the land of Israel was drowned
>   later in the war.
>
> The barn at Hammadia where I had loved was burned out.
> The sweet shop at Ein-Gedi was blown up by the enemy.
> The bridge at Ismailia, which I crossed to and fro on
> the even of my loves,
> has been torn to pieces.
>
> Thus my life is wiped out behind me according to an exact map:
>
> How much longer can my memories hold out?
>
> The girl from my childhood was killed and my father is dead.
>
> That's why you should never choose me
> to be a lover or a son, or a bridge-crosser
> or a citizen or a tenant.

It is no wonder, given the accumulated burden of these losses that the thirty-fourth poem goes on to move in three ascending sentences, from "Let the memorial hill remember, instead of me / that's his job" to

> let dust remember, let dung remember
> at the gate, let afterbirth remember.
>
> Let the wild beasts and the sky's birds eat and remember.
> Let all of them remember, so that I can rest.

At times the ravages of death and destruction almost reduce the poet to silence. But more often he posits two central consolations: the temporary joys and glories of erotic love (his typical procedure is to use the religious vocabulary of the Psalms to praise his beloved) and the sacred trust of memory. Love is for him a secular salvation, a doomed momentary stay against the furies of the outside world. So, too, remembering is a terrible and exhausting burden in his poems, but it is also one of his only redemptions. Memory itself becomes a hedge against oblivion. *Amen* is a book of faith and doubt, sorrow and sweetness, astonishment and recognition. But mostly it is a book of memory, a book that continues to remember even as it refuses that very act, even as it longs to rest. But there is no rest. Out of three or four in a room one is always standing at the window.

3

With the aid of Ted Hughes, Yehuda Amichai has translated his poems from Hebrew into English with surprising immediacy and effect. Many of the poems are written in a style that is disarmingly playful and direct, deceptively simple; they are so artful that at times they appear artless and naked, utterly spontaneous. What a long apprenticeship must precede such simplicity! Much of Amichai's strength rests in the tone and temper of that style, the way in which he strikes the exact registers of feelings, the sympathy that is always flowing outward in his work. Almost always his poems move on the winds of a rich and nearly surreal imagery, somehow both personal and anonymous, absolutely contemporary and yet very ancient. In a way the poems seem like one of the women they describe: "With a very short dress, in fashion / But weeping and laughter from ancient times."

Amichai is an especially tricky poet to translate. His characteristic linguistic strategy is to bring together in wry confrontation ancient biblical Hebrew and the living language of the streets. His poem "National Thoughts" speaks of a people's struggle to adapt a historical language to harsh contemporary realities:

> People caught in a homeland trap:
> to speak now in this weary language,
> a language that was torn from its sleep in the Bible: dazzled
> it wobbled from mouth to mouth. In a language that once described
> miracles and God, to say car, bomb, God.
>
> (*Selected Poetry*)

This modern Jacob-like struggle with the angel of Hebrew is one of the central issues of Amichai's work. It is also a compelling problem for anyone who chooses to translate him.

Unlike most books of contemporary poems, *Amen* is filled with other people. These poems speak with a natural and real tenderness of a village Jew ("God fearing and heavy eyed"), a tired gym teacher ("I never realized gym teachers could be sad"), a Czech refugee in London ("She behaves here as in a schoolbook for foreign languages"), and a bride without dowry ("What a terrible blood bath is she preparing for herself"). In a country filled with "all this false tourism" he speaks comically but also with a certain amount of warmth of "a Jewish girl / Who has American hope / In her eyes and whose nostrils are still / Very sensitive to anti-Semitism." And there is a heartrending poem about a schoolteacher who traveled all the way to New York to commit suicide.

People travel far away to say:
this reminds me of some other place.
That's like it was, it's similar. But
I know a man who traveled to New York
to commit suicide. He argued that the houses
in Jerusalem are not high enough and that everyone knows him.

I remember him with love, because once
he called me out of class in the middle of a lesson:
"There's a beautiful woman waiting for you outside in the
    garden,"
and he quieted the noisy children.

When I think about the woman and about the garden
I remember him on that high rooftop,
the loneliness of his death and the death of his loneliness.

Amichai's poems, as in this elegy for his schoolteacher, always try to keep "the route to childhood open." Often they speak with warmth, nostalgia, and reverence for his dead father. There are so many lovely lines about Amichai's father here (and "All those buried with him in one row, / His life's graduation class") that it is hard to resist quoting them all. One poem begins, "My father's cheeks when he was my age were soft / Like the velvet bag which held his praying shawl." And in "Letter of Recommendation" the son inside the lover breaks loose, and he cries out:

Oh, touch me, touch me, you good woman!
This is not a scar you feel under my shirt.
It's a letter of recommendation, folded, from my father:
"He is still a good boy and full of love."

I remember my father waking me up
for early prayers. He did it caressing
my forehead, not tearing the blanket away.

Since then I love him even more.
And because of this
let him be woken up
gently and with love
on the Day of Resurrection.

When Amichai speaks of childhood, he does so with a sly and wistful sadness, a longing to cross the barriers of that other. Cocteau tells us that "there are poets and grown ups." But at times Amichai almost takes Cocteau one step further, as if to say, "there is no such thing as a grownup" and, simultaneously, "we are all in exile from childhood." Lit up by a dry interior weeping, we are always recalling our lives, lugging around worn-out letters of recommendation from the past, our futile hearts, our endless queries for affection.

In Amichai's poems those queries are most often sent out as a lover. Sometimes his love songs ("Love Song," "Menthol Sweets," "Sometimes I Am Very Happy and Desperate") seem to be too short and unrealized, too imagistically interchangeable. But his finest love poems are filled with a bittersweet tenderness, an ancient mine of wisdom. He tells us that "He who put / masculine and feminine into the language put / into it also departing." Amichai is best, however, not when he laments a lost love but when he praises: simply, wildly, without restraint. "A Majestic Love Song," for example, begins majestically.

You are beautiful, like prophecies,
And sad, like those which come true,
Calm, with the calmness afterward.
Black in the white loneliness of jasmine,
With sharpened fangs: she-wolf and queen.

He is a poet able to speak of the royal scar and the blind golden scepter; he names a woman's rings as "the sacred leprosy of your fingers." It is only when the erotic poems move at the speed of such marvelous images that they earn their delicate vulnerability, their deep, heartbreaking voices. And from "You are beautiful, like the interpretation of ancient books" they move successfully into

> To live is to build a ship and a harbor
> at the same time. And to complete the harbor
> long after the ship was drowned.
>
> And to finish: I remember only
> that there was mist. And whoever
> remembers only mist—
> what does he remember?

Robert Lowell once called Randall Jarrell "the most heartbreaking poet of his generation." Amichai, too, is a heartbreaking and heartrending poet, and, in an odd way, in a different incarnation, speaking in different language of a different people moving through a different landscape, his poems sometimes remind me of Jarrell's finest and most luminous poems. Artfully simple, direct, and absolutely honest, simultaneously sweet and sorrowful, tender and unsentimental, both poets continually remember the enormous burden and mystery of ordinary adults shouldering their memories, carrying around the secret of their childhoods, the weight of their losses, the endless rituals of their daily lives, which are so utterly original, so utterly "commonplace and solitary." I would not push the connection, but I cannot shake the feeling that, however different they are, Jarrell's housewives, secretaries, and ball turret gunners are part of the same human band as Amichai's gym teachers, tourists, refugees, and Jewish soldiers. Both poets speak naturally of orphans, warriors, parents, children, and citizens.

Yehuda Amichai is a poet with a genuine talent for rendering the complex interior lives of other people. Human sympathy flows generously out of his work like a great river. He is, in his own small way, part of a tradition that dates at least as far back as the ancient Hebrew prophets. *Amen* is the book of a representative man with unusual gifts telling the tale of his tribe.

Donald Barthelme

Doubting It

It is inevitable but still disappointing that Donald Barthelme's fiction has suffered the kind of eclipse that always seems to follow a writer's death. A man dies, and suddenly his work is over, fully completed, posthumous. Nothing new will issue from his pen, and the world passes on. Readers turn elsewhere; students discover a couple of once-famous texts in a course on "Twentieth-Century Fiction" and wonder, perhaps, what the author was like; scholars go to work on the corpse, or "oeuvre." In Barthelme's case the entire postmodern aesthetic with which he was associated—remember the Fiction Collective?—has been eclipsed as well. Barthelme is often identified with his most radical fictions, and what once thrilled other prose writers, graduate students, and literary theorists—how he experimented with literary forms and dismantled the traditional short story— has come to seem passé. And yet there is an enormous gap between the reputation of Barthelme's work and the actual work itself. Forget about "metafiction" or "surfiction" or "superfiction" (all terms he disliked). He didn't have any particular enthusiasm for fiction about fiction, anyway. What he did have was an uncanny sense of how language has been put under terrific stress in our century, of how we all have entered into a "universe of discourse." There is no escaping that universe, except, perhaps, by dying.

To begin: Barthelme is an international figure. Go to your bookshelf and take down his two retrospective collections, *Sixty Stories* (1981) and *Forty Stories* (1987). Add the novels *Snow White*

This piece originally appeared as "On Donald Barthelme," *Triquarterly* (winter 1996/97), a publication of Northwestern University Press.

(1967) and *The Dead Father* (1975). There is a good deal more of value, but you now have in your hands the indispensable work of one of the true American heirs to Kafka and Borges.

After his death I wrote a memorial poem to a friend. I would now like to unpack that poem—a Barthelme-like exercise—in order to help the reevaluation of his work.

Apostrophe
(In Memory of Donald Barthelme, 1931–1989)

Perpetual worrier, patron of the misfit
and misguided, the oddball, the longshot,
irreverent black sheep in every family,
middle-aged man who languishes on the couch
with his head in his hands and often
spends the evening drinking by himself,
a dualist fated to deal in hybrids and cross-
breedings, riddles without answers, slumgullions,
impure waters, inappropriate longings, philosopher
of acedia, of spiritual torpor, nightsweats
and free-floating anxieties, sentencings,
sullenness in the face of existence, wry veteran
of the unresolved and the self-divided,
the besotted, the much married, defender
of the unhealthy and the uncommitted,
collagist of that mysterious overcrowded muck
we called a city, master of the solo riff
and the non sequitur, the call and response,
voice-overs and backtrackings, sublime bewilderments
and inexplicabilities, the comedy of post-
historical desires and thwarted passions,
first of the non-joiners, most unlikely,
tactful, and generous of fathers, you
who embarrassed the credulous and irritated
the unimaginative, who entertained the void
and recycled the dross, who deflated
the pretentious and deepened perplexities,
subject to odd stabbing rages of happiness,
weird bouts of pleasure, connoisseur of mornings,
of sunlight swinging into an open doorway,
small boys bumping into small girls, purposefully,
most self-conscious and ecstatic of ironists

who sang uncertainties like the Song of Songs
and dwelled in doubt like habitation,
my wary, unreachable, inconsolable friend,
I wish I believed in another world than this
so I could think of seeing you again
raising your wineglass to the Holy Ghost,
your "main man," and praising the mysteries,
Love and Work, looking down at the weather
which, as you said, is going to be fair
and warmer, warmer and fair, most fair.

Apostrophe

Apostrophe: "a digression in discourse; especially, a turning away from an audience to address an absent or imaginary person." This puts the reader—the audience—in the position of overhearing that address. John Stuart Mill said, "Eloquence is heard; poetry is overheard." W. B. Yeats modified this into "We make of the quarrel with others, rhetoric, but the quarrel with ourselves, poetry." Charlie Parker took the situation a step further by entirely turning his back on the audience. Donald Barthelme's work is also a turning away, a long quarrel with itself. He called the installments in that quarrel "stories."

(In Memory of Donald Barthelme, 1931–1989)

A postmodern elegy, an elegy for a postmodernist. A Homeric summoning, a sort of found poem that lifts phrases and sentences from Barthelme's work to create a portrait of him. The effect is in the cross-cuttings. The problem for the poet—indeed, the problem of all of Barthelme's work is what kind of language can one use when language itself is so debased in our time, so much of the problem. The ethic in his work is to go through—rather than around—the barriers of language.

"Donald Barthelme": the absent friend has now become an imaginary person, a name attached to a body of work. How to memorialize him? There is a parable by Kafka called not "The Tower of Babel" but "The Pit of Babel." Barthelme is a writer sentenced to digging a passage through that subterranean pit. That is one way of putting it. Here is another: he is known for his laconic wit and astonishing incongruities. But there is a secret in his work: he is heartbreaking.

Perpetual worrier . . .

He was a world-class worrier. I picture him like the speaker in his story "Chablis," sitting up in the early morning, at the desk on the second floor of the house, facing the street. It is 5:30, and he is "sipping a glass of Gallo Chablis with an ice cube in it, smoking, worrying." Most of his characters, mouthpieces all, are worrying about most things most of the time. The fact that they exaggerate their fears doesn't make them any less real. In truth, they are usually scared.

In *The Dead Father* Barthelme proposes that the "work ethic" should be replaced by the "fear ethic," and, in a sense, that's just what he has done in his own fiction. He writes of the terror of beginnings, the absence of middles, and the elusiveness of endings ("The Dolt"). The story "Morning" commences, "Say you're frightened. Admit it." The story "The Rise of Capitalism" concludes: "Fear is a necessary precondition to meaningful action. Fear is a great mover, in the end." Fear, like longing, is the engine that turns the world.

*. . . patron of the misfit
and misguided, the oddball, the longshot*

He had studied the melancholies, and he understood outsiders, being one himself. "What is wrong with me?" the narrator asks in one story: "Why am I not a more natural person, like my wife wants me to be?" All his characters are similarly afflicted. His work is filled with freakish figures whose natural habitat is alienation. The thirty-five-year-old man who absurdly finds himself in Mandible's elementary school class with eleven-year-olds is a good example. He cries out, "Let my experience here be that of the common run, I say; let me be, please God, typical" ("Me and Miss Mandible"). But of course that is not possible.

Another good example is Cecelia in "A City of Churches," who has come to Prester to open a car rental office. Everyone in town lives in a church of one sort or another, but Cecelia doesn't even have a denomination. What she does have is a secret.

> "I can will my dreams," Cecelia said. "I can dream whatever I want. If I want to dream that I'm having a good time, in Paris or

some other city, all I have to do is go to sleep and I will dream that dream. I can dream whatever I want."

"What do you dream, then, mostly?" Mr. Phillips said, looking at her closely.

"Mostly sexual things," she said. She was not afraid of him.

"Prester is not that kind of town," Mr. Phillips said, looking away.

Barthelme's characters are loyal to their dreams, their desires. They will not relinquish them for anything. They are afraid of themselves, but they will not be intimidated by others. They are heroes of longing.

irreverent black sheep in every family
I had gotten myself in trouble, and he said that he had once been a black sheep like me and that he would no doubt become one again. All black sheep have to stick together and help each other out, he said. He was reticent, but he was also kind. All writers are really black sheep, he said. A writing community is a whole flock of them.

In "Chablis" he remembers:

> I didn't go to church because I was a black sheep. There were five children in my family and the males rotated the position of black sheep among us, the oldest one being the black sheep for a while while he was in his DWI period or whatever and then getting grayer as he maybe got a job or was in the service and then finally becoming a white sheep when he got married and had a grandchild.

Barthelme's characters are ironic about everything, but especially about being respectable.

middle-aged man who languishes on the couch
with his head in his hand . . .
This is not just a matter of temperament. There is a philosophical position staked out by the non-joiner. Barthelme was a writer who always took a certain pride in distancing himself from reigning orthodoxies. He was a skeptic at heart. The theologian Brecker in the story "January" says that because you are not an

enthusiast "you languish on the couch with your head in your hands." This is a stance toward the world.

. . . and often
spends the evening drinking by himself
There were some (not all) evenings when the world seemed "fraught with the absence of promise." On those nights there was nothing to do "but go home and drink your nine drinks and forget about it" ("Critique de la Vie Quotidienne").

a dualist fated to deal in hybrids and cross-
breedings . . .
Barthelme was a moral writer. His morality consisted in turning everything inside out, in seeing everything as if in a reverse lens. He called himself "an incorrigibly double-minded man." This is to say he had a dialogic or double-minded imagination and tended to see everything in contradictory or irreconcilable terms. Thus the omnipresence of two conspiring voices in his work: the Q and A, the call and response, the open-ended dislocated conversation . . .

. . . riddles without answers . . .
"It is appropriate to pause and say that the writer is one who, embarking upon a task, does not know what to do."

"A writer, says Karl Krauss, is a man who can make a riddle out of an answer" ("Not-Knowing").

. . . slumgullions
He said:

> I'm fated to deal in mixtures, slumgullions, which preclude tragedy, which requires a pure line. It's a habit of mind, a perversity. Tom Hess used to tell a story, maybe from Lewis Carroll, I don't remember, about an enraged mob storming the palace shouting "More taxes! Less bread!" As soon as I hear a proposition I immediately consider its opposite. A double-minded man—makes for mixtures.

impure waters . . .
All the waters, but especially the linguistic ones, are polluted now. Barthelme understood this. He drank from the waters of Lethe and could not forget.

. . . inappropriate longings . . .

Barthelme greatly admired Walker Percy's book *The Second Coming*. In his *Paris Review* interview he said: "When the hero's doctors diagnosed *wahnsinnige Sehnsucht* or 'inappropriate longings' as what was wrong with him I like to fell off my chair. That's too beautiful to be real."

. . . philosopher of acedia, of spiritual torpor, nightsweats and free-floating anxieties . . .

In his last story "January," which is a kind of farewell performance in the form of a mock *Paris Review* interview, the theologian Thomas Brecker has written a dissertation on acedia. He explains:

> Acedia refuses certain kinds of relations with others. Of course there is a concomitant loss—of being with others, intersubjectivity. In literature, someone like Huysmans exemplifies the type. You could argue that he was just a 19th Century dandy of a certain kind but that misses the point, which is that something brought him to this position. As ever, fear comes into it. I argued that acedia was a manifestation of fear and I think that's true. Here it would be a fear of the need to submit, of joining the culture, of losing that much of the self to the culture.

We might say that in the course of Barthelme's work he progressed from irony to acedia. He started out by sending up the culture, but he ended in a state of spiritual torpor.

. . . sentencings

There is a doomed feeling about most, if not all, of his characters. Against which he poses his astonishing sentences, his endless interruptions, hesitations, qualifications, as in the seven-page story "Sentence," which is made up of a single sinuous, ardent, flexible sentence. It is a sentence, by the way, that does not end. The sentence is for Barthelme a terrific unit of meaning—a great, treasured, human construction. He used it to sing against the void.

sullenness in the face of existence . . .

Brecker says:

Acedia is often conceived of as a kind of sullenness in the face of existence; I tried to locate its positive features. For example, it precludes certain kinds of madness, crowd mania, it precludes a certain kind of error. You're not an enthusiast and therefore you don't go out and join a lynch mob.

. . . wry veteran
of the unresolved and the self-divided
Two characters are speaking. One quotes Kierkegaard: "Purity of heart is to will one thing." The other says:

—No. Here I differ with Kierkegaard. Purity of heart is, rather, to will several things, and not know which is the better, truer thing, and to worry about this forever. ("The Leap")

the besotted, the much married . . .
He was a romantic and a family man. The two did not always go together. "Holy Hell," a voice cries out in "Critique de la Vie Quotidienne": "Is there no end to this *family life?*"
No, there is not.
I am not the first to notice that the figures in Barthelme's stories are always lining up their drinks in an orderly row.
He can also declare: "Show me a man who has not married a hundred times and I'll show you a wretch who does not deserve God's good world" ("Overnight to Many Distant Cities"). If you are going to be loyal to other people, then you are going to have to be disloyal to acting out your own desires. And vice versa. There is a certain inevitable sadness attendant upon such a view. It is called "Civilization and Its Discontents."

. . . defender
of the unhealthy and the uncommitted
The speaker in "Chablis" watches the joggers, singly or in pairs, running "toward rude red health." He will not be one of them. He would rather smoke, drink, and worry.
"I was trying," Brecker points out, "to stake out a position for the uncommitted which still, at the same time, had something to do with religion."

Not many seem to recognize that theology was one of Barthelme's great subjects. His work is filled with theological longings. Brecker reports: "Heraclitus said that religion is a disease, but a noble one. I like that."

collagist . . .
Barthelme liked to play with typography. He enjoyed things that looked funny on the page, and he liked stories that included graphics ("Brain Damage," "At the Tolstoy Museum," "The Flight of Pigeons From the Palace"). This aspect of his work has inspired theorists and other practitioners of experimental fiction, but it mostly leaves me cold. More poignant, I think, is the way he juxtaposes sentences, punctures ideas, mixes dictions.

> —He who hath not love is a sad cookie.
> —This is the way, walk ye in it. Isaiah 30:21
>
> ("The Leap")

The art of juxtaposition allowed him to enact his double-mindedness. Collage became the action of planned incongruity.

> . . . *of that mysterious overcrowded muck*
we called a city . . .
In "City Life" Ramona playfully considers the nature of the city:

> —I have to admit we are locked in the most exquisite mysterious muck. This muck heaves and palpitates. It is multi-directional and has a mayor. To describe it takes many hundreds of thousands of words. Our muck is only part of a much greater muck— the nation-state—which is itself the creation of that muck of mucks, human consciousness.

It is this ur-muck, human consciousness, that is Barthelme's true subject. He needed a way to approach it. The city provided him with transportation.

> . . . *master of the solo riff*
and the non sequitur, the call and response,
voice-overs and backtrackings . . .

Barthelme learned from jazz how to make a statement, to place emphases within a statement and to introduce variations. He learned something about timing and pacing. He liked to riff, and the call and response appealed to his double-minded imagination. He could take fairly slender material and turn it in formally surprising ways. Hokie Mokie, the King of Jazz, is an homage to what he learned from music.

Michael Anania writes: "A good and useful—perhaps, even influential—article could be written on 'Music in Barthelme' . . . It would be a wondrously long list of lyrics quoted, operas mentioned, instruments described, concertos alluded to or even deliberately mangled."

The mangling is much to the point. In Barthelme's work we are always asked to consider and examine how each note—each sentence—follows upon the other. He distrusts smooth gliding. Hence the preponderance of non sequiturs in his work. He will go forward and then backward. He will let things float in from nowhere. And there is a kind of panic about the way that sequences falter: "The point of the story that came next was suddenly missing, I couldn't think of it" ("And Then"). He wrote, famously, that "Fragments are the only form I trust." And then he started distrusting fragments.

> *. . . sublime bewilderments*
and inexplicabilities . . .

Barthelme had great authority about his own lack of confidence in everything but especially in language as a transparent medium of thought. He said, "I believe that my every sentence trembles with morality in that each attempts to engage the problematic rather than to present a proposition to which all reasonable men must agree."

The sense of a stable self is repeatedly called into question in his work. Nothing is ever centered. The main character of "The Genius," for example, has continuous moments of self-doubt. He is always asking himself: "Am I really a—" or "What does it *mean* to be a—" or "Can one *refuse* to be a—?" Yes, one can.

> *. . . the comedy . . .*

Gregory Bateson has written that in our century humor is "the great alternative to psychosis." The supporting cast in Barthelme's working is always getting analyzed. The author is not. Humor is his weapon, his defense, his alternative to psychosis.

. . . of post-
historical desires and thwarted passions
Barthelme's characters are loyal to their own dissatisfactions. They won't agree to relinquish them. The fact that we mock our own unhappiness does not mean to deny that it exists, but it may make it a little more bearable. Here is the problem:

> What we really want in this world, we can't have. ("The Ed Sullivan Show")

> Well, Jacques said, we only do what we really want to do about eleven percent of the time. In our lives. ("City Life")

> What do you do with a patient who finds the world unsatisfactory? The world *is* unsatisfactory; only a fool would deny it. ("The Sandman")

first of the non-joiners . . .
A student once asked James Merrill what was the writer's responsibility to society, and he said, "Not to participate." That's the Barthelme position. In this author's diagnosis Saint Anthony's greatest temptation was "ordinary life." He himself would not be conscripted into it.

Charles Baxter writes:

> There is a certain stranded quality to the Barthelme protagonist, sitting in an easy chair at twilight with eleven martinis lined up in soldierly array. A fastidiousness, this is, and a humor about the shipwrecked condition, the orphaned longings, and something like an investigation of the possibilities inherent in melancholy. The heroes and heroines in this fiction are the not-joiners, the *non serviam* types. ("The Donald Barthelme Blues")

. . . most unlikely,
tactful, and generous of fathers . . .
The text is "A Manual for Sons" from *The Dead Father:*

> Many fathers did not wish, especially, to be fathers; the thing came upon them, seized them, by accident, or by someone else's

careful design, or by simple clumsiness on someone's part. Nevertheless, this class of father—the inadvertent—is often among the most tactful, light-handed, and beautiful of fathers.

Barthelme himself, of course, was this kind of father to many. He was the one who ironically, gracefully, and profoundly bore the burdens and shouldered the responsibilities. He did not make much of a point of it, though he did have a lovely sigh— weighty, humorous, world-weary. *"Fatherhood can be, if not conquered, at least 'turned down' in this generation."*

. . . you
who embarrassed the credulous and irritated
the unimaginative . . .
Barthelme could arouse a great fury in unsympathetic readers. His editor at the *New Yorker,* Roger Angell, has said: "Many readers had difficulty at first cottoning to writing like this. They were put off by Barthelme's crosscutting and by his terrifying absence of explanation, and those who resisted him in the end may have been people who were by nature unable to put their full trust in humor."

. . . who entertained the void
Barthelme said that Beckett's work is "an embarrassment to the void." It's true of his own work as well. Except he tried not only to embarrass the void but also to entertain it. See "The School" and "Nothing: A Preliminary Account."

and recycled the dross . . .
One of his chief means of verbal entertainment was to recycle our cultural junk, or verbal garbage, what William Gass called "the leading edge of the trash phenomenon." Modern culture is wildly unmasked in his work, especially in his early stories. There's a smart-alecky tone to stories in which he sends up, say, television or the language of existentialism or the commodification of nearly everything. A famous example comes from "The Indian Uprising": "People were trying to understand. I spoke to Sylvia. 'Do you think this is a good life?' The table held apples, books, long-playing records. She looked up. 'No.' "

Christopher Lasch writes: "A latter-day Madame Bovary,

Snow White is a typical victim of mass culture, the culture of commodities and consumerism."

Many of the sociological features of Barthelme's work leave me unmoved, but it is a different story when he writes about contemporary unhappiness, when we are asked "to consider for instance the area of real-time online computer-controlled wish evaporation." There is a lot of verbal snap and sparkle in Barthelme's work. He has a gift for deflation and an ear for clichés. But the tone darkens whenever he talks about the sadness of wish evaporation in real time. Then he is singing back to the sirens.

> . . . *who deflated*
> *the pretentious and deepened perplexities*

Barthelme's scrupulous irony is deflating. It gave him no rest. Pompousness cannot stand up to it. His work deepens our sense of what we don't know. Some people can't bear to have answers turned back into questions.

> *subject to odd stabbing rages of happiness,*
> *weird bouts of pleasure, connoisseur of mornings,*
> *of sunlight swinging into an open doorway,*
> *small boys bumping into small girls, purposefully*

Barthelme's work is animated by instances of supreme happiness and well-being, moments of radiance. There are times when he is overwhelmed by gaiety. He praises a simple soup "in an ecstasy of admiration." He praises the splendid voices of Bessie Smith, Alice Babs, Joan Armatrading, and Aretha Franklin.

> —Each voice testifying to the greater honor and glory of God, each in its own way.
> —Damn straight.
>
> ("The Leap")

He makes up lists of pleasures: from a jug of wine to a walk in the park. He praises a day when "the singing sunlight turns you every way but loose" and, later, you "accidentally notice the sublime." One of his favorite subjects, of course, is "small boys bumping into small girls, purposefully." It is always a wedding day, a plain day, a day to remember.

most self-conscious and ecstatic of ironists
who sang uncertainties like the Song of Songs
Barthelme could be oddly ecstatic about the writer's impossible uphill struggle. He wrote:

> How joyous the notion that, try as we may, we cannot do other than fail and fail absolutely, and that the task will remain always before us, like a meaning for our lives. ("Nothing: A Preliminary Account")

He also said in an interview: "In this century there's been much stress placed not upon what we know but on knowing that our methods are themselves questionable—our Song of Songs is the Uncertainty Principle."

One could not say that this made him happy, exactly. But he did consider irony "useful" and even "necessary."

> *A:* But I love my irony.
> *B:* Does it give you pleasure?
> *A:* A poor . . . A rather unsatisfactory . . .
> *B:* The unavoidable tendency of everything particular to emphasize its own particularity.
> *A:* Yes.
>
>   ("Kierkegaard Unfair to Schlegel")

Barthelme relished Kierkegaard's idea that an irony directed against the whole of existence produces "estrangement and poetry."

and dwelled in doubt like a habitation
He made doubt his residence. That is his ethic and his aesthetic. His best essay on writing is called "Not-Knowing." He liked to point out that the very nature of artistic activity is failure. In "The Sandman" a fellow writes a letter, somewhat inappropriately, to his girlfriend's shrink. He says:

> Let me point out, if it has escaped your notice, that what an artist does, is fail. Any reading of the literature (I mean the theory of artistic creation), however summary, will persuade you instantly that the paradigmatic artistic experience is that of failure. The actualization fails to meet, equal, the intuition. There is

something "out there" which cannot be brought "here." This is standard. I don't mean bad artists, I mean good artists. There is no such thing as a "successful artist" (except, of course, in worldly terms). The proposition should read, "Susan becomes an artist and lives unhappily every after." This is the case. Don't be deceived.

Barthelme vowed to be one of what Philip Larkin called "the less deceived." It's a painful position but one with integrity.

my wary, unreachable, inconsolable friend

> *Wary:* "on one's guard; cautious, watchful."
> *Unreachable:* Not to be reached.
> *Inconsolable:* "Incapable of being consoled or solaced; despondent."
> *Friend:* "One with whom one is allied in a struggle or cause; a comrade."

I wish I believed in another world than this
Barthelme would have liked to believe in a world beyond our own. This was denied him. The theologian Brecker confesses: "I can do without certitude. I would have liked to have had faith."

As a writer Barthelme could be very funny—and deadly serious—about the death of God. His favorite tactic was to take theological questions completely literally, as in "The death of God left the angels in a strange position" ("On Angels") or:

> —Today we make the leap of faith. Today.
> —Today?
> —Today.
> —We're really going to do it? At last?
> —Spent too much time fooling around. Today we do it.
> —I don't know. Maybe we're not ready?
> —I am cheered by the wine of possibility and the growing popularity of light. Today's the day.
> —You're serious.
> —Intensely. First, we examine our consciences.
>
> ("The Leap")

After examining his conscience, however, this speaker, this free-floating voice—we can't really call him a character—

decides that he can't quite make the leap of faith. Why not? Because he is a "double-minded man." He would try another day. He would fail again.

so I could think of seeing you again
We were in Rome. We had just had a terrific lunch. With pasta in cream sauce, with lots of wine. We took a long walk, since it was one of those days when the singing sunlight turns you every way but loose. He was going home in the morning. "So long, see you but not tomorrow," I said, ever the glib one. "See you, but not in Paradise."

raising your wineglass to the Holy Ghost,
your "main man" . . .
He liked to call the Holy Ghost his "main man." At the end of the story "Overnight to Many Distant Cities" he actually imagined having a meal with the Holy Ghost. It was a great success.

> Lunching with the Holy Ghost I praised the world, and the Holy Ghost was pleased. "We have that little problem in Barcelona," He said, "the lights go out in the middle of dinner." "I've noticed," I said. "We're working on it," He said, "what a wonderful city, one of our best." "A great town," I agreed.

> . . . *and praising the mysteries,*
Love and Work . . .
Love is one of Barthelme's recurrent, driving subjects. He can be very wry about it, especially concerning the love between men and women. He writes: "Love, which is a kind of permission to come closer than ordinary norms of good behavior might usually sanction." And: "Which enables us to see each other without clothes on, for example, in lust and shame." And: "Which allows us to say wounding things to each other which would not be kosher under the ordinary rules of civilizing discourse." Nevertheless: "He who hath not love is a sad cookie."

Love is also connected to writing, to work. "The story ends," he writes in "Rebecca": "It was written for several reasons. Nine of them are secrets. The tenth is that one should never cease considering human love. Which remains as grisly and golden as ever, no matter what is tattooed upon the warm tympanic page."

> *. . . looking down at the weather,*
> *which, as you said, is going to be fair*
> *and warmer, warmer and fair, most fair.*

There is a hopefulness that somehow breaks through the melancholy in Barthelme's work. It is one of his moods. "Tomorrow, fair and warmer," he writes in "Overnight to Many Distant Cities," "warmer and fair, most fair . . ." There is also the happiness of his extravagant imagination fulfilled. There is an odd stabbing pleasure in reading his work. "The war is temporary," Paul Klee declares in one story: "But drawings and chocolate go on forever."

To Wrestle an Angel

After twenty penitential years in Mesopotamia Jacob was hastily returning to Canaan, land of his birth, where he hoped to be reconciled with his twin brother, Esau, whose birthright and blessing he had taken so long ago. They would meet face to face. Picture Jacob (Yaakov) on the horizon—the reflective and wily one, the stealthy intellectual in the family, the cunning younger son grown up and traveling home like a prosperous tribal chief with his two wives, Leah and Rachel (one plain and one beautiful), two maids (Zilpah and Bilhah), eleven sons (the future of Israel itself), a host of servants, and large sturdy flocks of animals. The procession wound along a route east of the Jordan River. When Jacob learned Esau was advancing with a force of four hundred men, he divided everyone and everything into two companies; he appealed directly to the Lord ("Pray save me from the hand of my brother . . ."); and he sent ahead gifts of animals in successive droves to try to appease him. Here was one more reminder Jacob was still guilty and guileful, still fearful of his brother's righteous enmity. The mind boggles at what Esau must have thought as he saw them approaching—one wave after the next, a veritable tide of goats and kids, ewes and rams, nursing camels and their young, cows and bulls, male and female asses.

Jacob set camp, but that night he suddenly arose and took his family across the ford of the Jabbok. Then he took his possessions and sent them across. He was left alone, and in the darkness a man came and wrestled with him until daybreak. Jacob

---

Originally published as "The Story of Jacob's Wrestling with an Angel," in *Genesis: As It Is Written,* ed. David Rosenberg (San Francisco: Harper San Francisco, 1996).

did not falter, not even when the stranger dislocated his thigh. At daybreak the unknown assailant grew desperate:

> And he said, Let me go, for the day breaketh. And he said, I will not let thee go, except thou bless me.
> And he said unto him, What *is* thy name? And he said, Jacob.
> And he said, Thy name shall be called no more Jacob, but Israel: for as a prince hast thou power with God and with men, and hast prevailed.
> And Jacob asked *him*, and said, Tell *me*, I pray thee, thy name. And he said, Wherefore *is* it *that* thou dost ask after my name? And he blessed him there.
> And Jacob called the name of the place Peniel: for I have seen God face to face, and my life is preserved. (King James Version, 32.26–30)

Jacob's encounter with an unknown assailant is a story of majestic strangeness. The Yahwist who dramatized this episode, perhaps some time around the tenth century B.C.E., was first and foremost not a theologian but a lyricist and a storyteller. As a poet, I have returned often, even obsessively, to this jarring scene. I have turned to it for inspiration but also to try to learn precisely how the Yahwist managed to pack and convey Jacob's encounter with divinity. I have sometimes imagined the Yahwist as a kind of Virgilian guide who could lead me through the mysteries as I have struggled to dramatize the epiphanic and visionary experiences of others, especially of writers I care about deeply. This was most evident to me in writing *Earthly Measures*. For example, I looked to the Yahwist as a model when I was writing a set of three pieces—"From a Train," "Unearthly Voices," and "The Renunciation of Poetry"—about a trip that Hugo von Hofmannsthal took to Greece in 1908. These lyrics comprise a modernist triptych that progresses from the moment divinity asserts itself to the historical instant when the gods turn into a single God to a time when divinity seeps out of tangible things. The Yahwist's exemplary imagination also aided me in another poem, "The Watcher," about Leopardi's experience in Rome in 1823, a lyric in which I tried to substantiate the sense of *nulla,* or nothingness. And I looked to the Yahwist for guidance as I wrote "Away from Dogma," a poem that dramatizes Simone Weil's three mystical contacts with God. Here she is in Assisi:

She disliked the Miracles in the Gospels.
She never believed in the mystery of contact,
here below, between a human being and God.
She despised popular tales of apparitions.

But that afternoon in Assisi she wandered
through the abominable Santa Maria degli Angeli
and happened upon a little marvel of Romanesque
purity where St. Francis liked to pray.

She was there a short time when something absolute
and omnivorous, something she neither believed
nor disbelieved, something she understood—
but what was it?—forced her to her knees.

I have tried to learn from the Yahwist how to retain the mystery at the heart of the hieratic confrontation with an unknown or supernatural force. It may be understood retrospectively but cannot be naturalized or explained away. Jacob's experience is akin to dreams and visions yet is presented by the writer as an event that actually happens. In this regard the author is something of a Kafkaesque dissembler, a purveyor of the uncanny. Everything is presented as literal. The unknown assailant knows the etymology of Yaakov's name (*heel-holder*), a play on the fact that Jacob had emerged from the womb grasping the heel of his brother Esau. The stranger also gives him a farewell blessing. But this was a common social interaction at the time and didn't require resorting to angels. It was more unusual for the stranger to rename him "Israel," which may mean "God-fighter" or "May God protect." Even so, it was outrageous for Jacob to turn around and claim to have been face to face with God, since at the time it was commonly accepted that to see God face to face was to die. Jacob saw God and lived. This revelation was startling, violent, jolting—a leap of faith. That's how the Yahwist chose to create and define the ecstatic religious experience. And that's how it would reverberate down through the centuries.

I read Jacob's experience through a literary lens, and for me it is connected to what Wordsworth termed "spots of time." It resembles Virginia Woolf's "moments of being" and James Joyce's "epiphanies." Such moments are by definition sudden, unexpected, and apocalyptic. They have a rupturing intensity that is deep and troubling, even terrifying. They are triggered by external events, but they cannot be anticipated or entirely explained in rational terms. Indeed, they create a gap or wide hole in experience as the social world dissolves and the visible world is usurped. One world is suppressed as another is encountered. The epiphanic moment always marks a crisis point in a work, a threshold experience. It signals a dramatic turning point for the protagonist, who is deeply changed by the experience. He may even be so shocked that he emerges from it claiming a new name, a new identity. Or claiming that he has seen God face to face.

I think it was when I saw Claude Lorrain's evocative night landscape in Leningrad, in 1973, that I fully understood how indispensable the nocturnal setting is to reading Jacob's story. Textual scholars have pointed to the great antiquity of a tale that bears many resemblances to oral sagas in which a hero struggles against a local river spirit who must be placated or defeated to obtain a crossing. Folklore abounds with tales of ghosts and spirits who, like the figure of Hamlet's father, must slink away before daybreak. The Yahwist uses this tradition to create a spiritually transforming experience in writing. Psychologically, everything must happen under the eerie cover of darkness because Jacob's experience is unsightly, epiphanic, and prophetic, an event out of time. The linear flow and narrative momentum of the overarching story—Jacob's return to his homeland and reconciliation with his brother—is radically interrupted; indeed, what we think of as chronological or historical time is completely ruptured on this night of nights. The event is initiated by two crossings as Jacob sends everyone and everything to the other side of the tributary, in effect doubly separating himself from the social realm—the world of familiars, world of possessions. He is enacting a poetic crossing, dispossessing himself of his former character. He is now a solitary traveler left on the edge of a deep gorge. The nocturnal setting is so crucial because he has moved outside the arena of what can be apprehended by daylight and entered the realm of the visionary. He has moved from eyesight to vision. The dangerous encounter that follows is the pivotal moment—the turning point—in Jacob's life. The great archaic genius of the Yahwist was to literalize in a human figure the encounter with the Otherworld.

One should keep in mind that Jacob struggles with a man whose identity is unknown to him. He only later takes the stranger to have been a divine emissary. The ambiguity is crucial. It is preemptive to capitalize the word *Man* (as the Living Bible does), and it somehow misses the point to label the section in advance "Jacob Wrestles with God" (as the New International Bible does). A great deal of ink has been spilled trying to identify Jacob's angelic assailant—the candidates include Michael, Gabriel, and many others—but the *elohim* who blesses Jacob resolutely refuses to identify himself. He will not give away his own name. Jack Miles has recently pointed out that virtually all the commentaries follow Jacob's own retrospective interpretation of the event, though the Yahwist leaves tantalizingly open the question of whether or not Jacob ever actually sees the face of the man who disappears at daybreak. And yet there is also an overwhelming warrant in Jacob's entire saga for understanding the struggle as a supernatural encounter. It was foreshadowed in his competitive grappling with Esau in the womb. It resulted in the naming of a nation.

To understand Jacob's encounter I would additionally apply a brilliant rabbinical comment from the *Bereshit Rabba* (chap. 1) that Maimonides cites in *Guide for the Perplexed:* "To Abraham, whose prophetic power was great, the angels appeared in the form of men; to Lot, whose prophetic power was weak, they appeared as angels." The prophet's power is greatest when he can read the signs of divinity. One might even say that at Bethel Jacob was still like Lot, a lesser prophet, when he had a dream of angels going up and down a stairway that stretched between earth and heaven. He was something of a stronger prophet at the place he named Mahanaim ("This is God's camp!"), when the messengers of the Lord actually met him on the way, though still appearing to him as angels. It was only at Peniel, where he was put to the supreme test, that he truly became like Abraham, a great visionary, a fully conscious prophet; he wrestled with a man and knew him to be an angel.

I think of Jacob as an agonist of the sublime, a person lamed while seizing the transcendental blessing. His nocturnal encounter was an aspiration for the power of the spirit, a terrifying quest for divine vitality. In the superb first volume of his tetralogy *Joseph and His Brothers,* Thomas Mann describes Jacob's en-counter as "a frightful, heavy, highly sensual dream, yet with a certain wild sweetness; no light and fleeting vision that passes and is gone, but a dream of such physical warmth, so dense with actuality, that it left a double legacy of life behind it." The story has such great resonance for poets and prose writers, I think, because writing itself is an encounter with the unknown, a hard struggle with the unsaid, the unsayable. The lyric poem especially is a raid on the mysteries, an attempt to wrestle meaning out of silence. To write is to stand on the edge of a dark gorge guarded by a mysterious stranger. "The written page is no mirror," Edmond Jabès has asserted: "Writing means confronting an unknown face." Jacob may embrace the angel, but for me that embrace must also be agonistic, since it is an uncanny confrontation with the unknown, the unknowable. Writing is psychologically dangerous because it means putting oneself at risk. In his poem "Der Angel" Rilke writes of the hands of a being who comes to visit you at night "to test you with a fiercer grip" and "seize you as if they were creating you." They would "break you out of your mould." Like Jacob, writers have always been intent on wresting divinity from demonic hands.

The making of poems is for me both an agonizing and an exhilarating experience. The agony comes because it is so infernally difficult to get something right in words, to substantiate something elusive and intuitive. It's hard to make language answerable to experience—indeed, an experience in and of itself—especially when the experience one is writing about is inchoate or even mystical. But art is also a form of problem solving, and I have most often tried to stave off doubts about one's enterprise with an obsessive concentration on what Pound called luminous details. What a pleasure, for example, to saturate myself in Simone Weil's writings, especially in her "Spiritual Autobiography," where she describes her three mystical contacts with God. Absorption is happiness, and it makes writing—especially the writing of lyric poems—akin to prayer. Weil called prayer "unmixed attention," and George Herbert described it as "something understood." The exhilaration in writing comes in getting something right, creating a new thing in words, something absorbed and understood.

I can only describe the experience of writing poems metaphori-cally because it is for me a spiritual as well as a literary enter-prise. I'd like to tease out the imaginative implications of that enterprise by associating what happened to Jacob at Peniel with what García Lorca called "duende." The duende was an Anda-lusian trickster figure, a sprite something like the Yiddish *dyb-buk,* but in his essay "Play and Theory of the Duende" Lorca radically enlarged it into a figure for artistic inspiration. In Lorca's terms the duende becomes a demonic presence, a scorched (and scorching) spirit, "a mysterious power which everyone senses and no philosopher explains" (Goethe). "All that has black sounds has duende," Lorca said.

Lorca distinguished between the duende, the muse, and the angel, but he thought of the muse as a figure who dictates and prompts from afar, and he considered the angel a dazzling light-filled being who flies overhead. He imagined angels as saintly figures who guide and defend, announce and forewarn. None come to attack. Therefore, he thought, "the true fight is with the duende." Yet Jacob's encounter with an unnamed *elohim* is closer to the struggle Lorca attributed to the duende. This struggle is shadowed by mortality. It is anguished, disconsolate, and takes place in a country open to death. Harold Bloom is surprisingly close to this idea when he nominates the Angel of Death as Jacob's unknown antagonist. The duende wounds, Lorca said, and fights the creator on the rim of a well, much as the elohim marks and permanently injures Jacob on the rim of a gorge. "In the healing of that wound, which never closes," Lorca wrote, "lies the invented, strange qualities of a man's work."

The spirit who wounds and blesses can be taken as a meta-phor for the quest to create something lasting from the catastro-phe of one's character. Like the ancients, the poet hopes that a new name will bring about a transformation of the self, a new identity. After all, Jacob's new name suggested that he was no longer a supplanter, a heel holder, but one "who strives with God" (Hosea). The scandal of poetic originality is that the birth of something new is always unsightly; the work comes from a dark, relentless, internal, at times even demented, struggle. At times uncertainty itself seems like a literary birthright, unceas-ing effort a calling. "Je est un autre," Rimbaud said: "I is an-other." Stealth is required—and courage—when the very self is estranged, especially since one hopes to emerge with a new name, a consoling gift.

I think of writing poetry as a way of forcing a blessing—a creative exuberance, a ringing ecstasy—from the depths of the unknown. The lyric poem is a trope against time, almost a form of religious enthusiasm. Shelley, an apostle of the visionary imagination, said that "poetry redeems from decay the visitations of the divinity in man." That seems to me an idea worthy of Jacob's sublime encounter. To bring a poem into the world is to feel in a small way in the presence of something sacred, something blessed. Writing is a way of engaging the mysteries. To be like Jacob one must wrestle all night with a stranger and know him to be an angel. One must struggle with an unknown, unnamed fate and then go forth in the morning, wounded, thankful, and refreshed.

My Grandfather's Poems

My grandfather died when I was eight years old. He was sixty-four. I remember him as tall and thin, slightly stooped and round shouldered, gentle, unobtrusive, and formal in his manner—a man, as Isaac Babel wrote, with spectacles on his nose and autumn in his heart. For as long as I can remember, everyone in my family said that I resembled him; photographs show that we have the same long face: dark, stubborn, hawklike. My grandmother used to throw up her arms in mock dismay at our apparent similarities. It was rotten luck that both her husband and her grandson were willful and impractical, a hopeless combination, two typically male Ginsburg traits. Thank heavens she had shown the good sense to deliver two daughters.

My *zaydee* always wore a plain dark suit and a slightly faded gray hat. We never saw him dressed informally; he wore a stiff white shirt and a dark tie even on those rare occasions when he accompanied our family to the beach, even when he came to babysit for my sister and me on Saturday evenings. We loved when he visited. He brought us small pleasurable gifts—a sky-blue dreidel, an elaborate puzzle with thick Hebrew letters, a pocketful of Hershey Kisses—and allowed us to stay up nearly as late as we wanted. He never scolded us, no matter what we did. Sometimes he read us stories or sang Yiddish songs in a low, tearing whisper. He taught us word games. He hugged us. Always he kissed me on each arm before he sent me to bed for the night.

After my grandfather had a heart attack, my mother used to bring my sister and me to the hospital to see him. We weren't taken to his room—we were apparently too young to visit—but to the parking lot across the street from the hospital. He would

Originally appeared in *Stand* (summer 1986) and was reprinted in *Conversant Essays* (Detroit: Wayne State University Press, 1990).

walk to the window and wave to us from the seventh floor. We stood on the hood of the car and waved back—wildly, fervently. It was a kind of game; we'd continue waving until he'd finally get too tired and return to bed. The last time we saw him, he leaned over and pressed his lips against the window. The next day he was dead.

My mother idolized her father—as he must have adored her; after he died my grandfather was very much kept alive in our house. He was an affectionate memory, a constant human model, an old-world idea. In local family terms he had become his admirers, as Auden said of Yeats: in this case, my mother and my aunt. He was soft-spoken, loving, intellectual; he was passionate about politics (a devotee of Franklin Roosevelt, a fervent Zionist) and loved books, especially history books. My father called these memories "a portrait of my grandfather," recognizable but softened around the edges.

For the last decade of his life Grandpa earned his living, such as it was, by selling clothes on Maxwell Street. He despised his job. He was as poorly suited to being a salesman as one could imagine. The family consensus was that the great professional mistake of his life had been to drop out of dental school after his father had died. His largest personal mistake may have been to marry my grandmother, his opposite in every way. Grandpa was softhearted, impractical, nostalgic, and European; grandma was hardheaded, pragmatic, forward looking, American. He liked reading; she preferred playing cards.

It took my grandmother five years to agree to marry my grandfather. She liked the way that he courted her—with chocolate and books, with fine old-fashioned manners—but there was something unworldly about him that bothered her. She was well into her thirties before she finally consented. My grandfather was selling *The Book of Knowledge* at the time and had tucked away a little money. But the market for encyclopedias plunged along with the stock market, and so my grandfather moved his wife and daughter to Rochester to take over what had once been his father's dry goods business. It failed within months. He invested in a new kosher delicatessen but lost all his money within the year (he refused to make illegal payments to the local rabbis—the source of his boundless contempt for the clergy—and was too shy to ask his partner to stop cheating him). Eventually, he moved his wife and two daughters to Chicago. For years after that he traveled through the Midwest as a stringer for the Yiddish newspaper, *The Day* (*Der Yidishe Tog*). He traveled eleven months of every year, writing small unsigned pieces for what the masthead called "the newspaper of the Yiddish intelligentsia." I have often wondered what it was like for him to track down stories of "Jewish" interest in cities like Ottumwa and Cedar Falls. He liked the job, but, after he suffered his first heart attack, he could no longer travel and was forced to work in the city. That's when he went to work on Maxwell Street. Despite his exemplary character, those last years were often held up to me as a negative model: don't be like your grandpa, become a professional, succeed.

Sometime during my childhood I discovered that my grandfather was a poet—or, at least, that he was always scribbling poems on the backs of envelopes or on small white pieces of paper. I'm not sure how I gleaned this information, since I was never actually told about it. I don't think I ever read or saw one of his poems either. But the idea must have struck deep bottom and anchored—something half-remembered, half-forgotten, out of the distant past. The first adult poem I remember consciously reading was "The Lady of Shalott." I found it in a worn anthology on a moldy shelf in the basement. For some reason I vaguely assumed my grandfather had written it. I never mentioned this to anyone, but I was proud of the beautiful high-sounding language the poem commanded. It sent me into sweet reverie.

It wasn't until I began to write my first poems years later that I began to think about my grandfather's poems again. Where were they? What were they like? What happened to them? I pestered my grandmother; I questioned my mother and my aunt. No one knew; no one seemed to know anything about those poems, except that they were written in Yiddish. Or were they written in Hebrew? Oh yes, he composed them all right but never actually read them to anyone. He used to fold them and tuck them away between the pages of his books. Sometimes he wrote them directly on the inside covers of his Hebrew books. Where were his books then? My grandmother had given them away to a local charity after his death. Which charity? She couldn't remember; she couldn't understand why I cared so much. They were scattered by now. What did it matter? I couldn't believe she had given his books away, his books! What was she supposed to do, she asked with sudden contempt, keep them forever? Yes! I shouted back. You're crazy, she said, shaking her head with disapproval: you're as crazy as your grandfather. The conversation was over. My grandfather's poems had vanished forever.

No one ever thought to keep any of my grandfather's writing. No one missed his poems, or even wondered what they were about. Everyone in the family was aware that he wrote poetry—at least that's what they thought he was doing—but writing was considered something quirky that he liked to do, his particular form of amusement, like playing solitaire on long winter nights. It was also a sign of his estrangement from the mercantile world, from the realm of business—from success. That's one of the reasons my parents were so concerned when I began writing poems. My larger family treated the whole idea of poetry with faint distaste, as if I had contracted something unpleasant that I would hopefully outgrow, like acne. Even then I knew they associated writing poems with poverty, sadness, and failure, with the realities of my grandfather's life. I also recognized that my mother was just the tiniest bit pleased; I was, indeed, her father's grandson.

I have imagined my grandfather's poems many years now. They are always before me, an unnamed presence, a spiritual ideal. I recognize now that the voice I have discovered in other Eastern European poets is my grandfather's: by turns wry, tender, passionate, playful, modest, heartfelt; the voice of a quiet intellectual who understands that he lives inside history, who tries to speak with true feeling. Whenever I see a photograph of a Czech or a Hungarian Jewish poet, a Jirí Orten or a Miklós Radnóti, I think about my grandfather again. I wonder if his poems approached the strata of theirs: personal, outspoken, learned, heartbreaking. I imagine my grandfather's voice when Orten addresses God as "a bully who took away so much" or when Radnóti cries out in tender desperation, "Oh you who love me, love me bravely!" I consider my grandfather's life again when Marina Tsvetaeva claims that in a gentile world "all poets are Jews." I think about him, too, when I read Yehuda Amichai's affirmation that we are all "festive weepers, etching names on every stone, touched by hope, hostages of governments and history, blown by wind and gathering holy dust."

UNDER DISCUSSION
David Lehman, General Editor
Donald Hall, Founding Editor

Volumes in the Under Discussion series collect reviews and essays about
individual poets. The series is concerned with contemporary American and
English poets about whom the consensus has not yet been formed and the
final vote has not been taken. Titles in the series include: